Building Cooperative
Movements in
Developing Countries

PRAEGER SPECIAL STUDIES IN
INTERNATIONAL ECONOMICS AND DEVELOPMENT

Building Cooperative Movements in Developing Countries

THE SOCIOLOGICAL AND PSYCHOLOGICAL ASPECTS

Konrad Engelmann

FREDERICK A. PRAEGER, Publishers
New York · Washington · London

The purpose of the Praeger Special Studies is to make specialized re-search monographs in U.S. and international economics and politics available to the academic, business, and government communities. For further information, write to the Special Projects Division, Frederick A. Praeger, Publishers, 111 Fourth Avenue, New York, N.Y. 10003.

FREDERICK A. PRAEGER, PUBLISHERS
111 Fourth Avenue, New York, N.Y. 10003, U.S.A.
5, Cromwell Place, London S.W. 7, England

Published in the United States of America in 1968
by Frederick A. Praeger, Inc., Publishers

Library of Congress Catalog Card Number: 68-55002

Printed in the United States of America

FOR ILSE

PREFACE

For many years, the author was an active participant in cooperative movements in developed and developing countries. Through personal experience, he
acquired information and made observations that he
hopes will be of interest to others who are helping
emerging nations develop their resources and improve
their standard of living. By describing his experiences, he hopes to make a modest contribution to international collaboration and understanding and, at
the same time, to express his appreciation to those
who gave him an opportunity to participate in one of
the greatest aid projects of this era.

Before becoming involved in cooperative work, the
author lived for nearly ten years in a Middle Eastern
country, where he became familiar with the difficulties of adapting non-Western social and economic
structures to Western standards. Later, as head of
the Foreign Relations Department of the Central Association of German Rural Cooperatives, he had the
broadening experience of numerous contacts with visitors from developing regions who came to study cooperative principles and methods and to learn how to
apply them to their own countries. This led to prolonged trips to emerging nations, to frequent participation in international cooperative meetings, and
to the leadership of seminars for cooperative leaders
from developing countries.

The cooperative form of organization is a highly
flexible vehicle for furthering common planning and
action by affecting individuals more intensively than
other forms of organization. It requires careful consideration of historical, social, and economic conditions. Recognition of this has led the author to
emphasize the sociological and psychological aspects
of cooperative undertakings in less developed countries. This book is not merely reportage. Sociology
and psychology are complex subjects, open to various

vii

interpretations. Thus, some parts of the book may appear to be rather subjective, and some conclusions may be labeled "unscientific." Yet the author hopes that he has succeeded in the main in extracting the essential objective facts from admittedly subjective sources.

The research material was extensive enough to allow comparisons between reports and to adjust data that might have reflected irregular conditions and could have led to one-sided or nonessential conclusions. Reports from many developing countries that were presented to conferences and seminars under the author's leadership or produced in collaboration with representatives of emerging nations formed the basic documentation. In addition, there were numerous minutes, protocols, and notes written during or immediately after meetings, discussions, and private interviews. This basic material was supplemented by publications of such international agencies as the Food and Agriculture Organization of the United Nations (FAO) in Rome and the International Labor Office (ILO) in Geneva. Both organizations have been most helpful in the preparation of this book.

Several U.S. Government agencies, as well as some of the leading cooperative institutions, have also provided considerable information. Repeated conferences with representatives of public and private organizations dealing with cooperative establishments all over the world, plus visits to educational and other institutions connected with these organizations, were of equally great help. The Farmer Cooperative Service of the U.S. Department of Agriculture, the Agency for International Development, the International Projects Department of the National Farmers Union, the Cooperative League of the U.S.A., the Program of Cooperatives Department of Social Affairs of the Organization of American States, the CUNA (formerly Credit Union National Association) International, and the International Cooperative Training Center at the University of Wisconsin assisted and encouraged the author in so many ways that their contributions cannot be overstated.

The Fund for the Promotion of Cooperative Research and Science, administered by the Central Bank of German Cooperatives (Deutsche Genossenschaftskasse in Frankfurt, Germany), helped offset the expense of preparing a first edition of this book, which was written and published in Germany. The present book is a completely revised and considerably enlarged version of the original, updated to include reports of 1966 and 1967.

CONTENTS

Page

PREFACE   vii

LIST OF ABBREVIATIONS   xiii

Chapter

1   POLITICO-HISTORICAL AND SOCIOECONOMIC
    FACTORS IN DEVELOPING COUNTRIES   1

        Note to Chapter 1   21

2   MOTIVATIONS, GOALS, AND OBSTACLES
    FOR COOPERATIVE ESTABLISHMENTS   22

        Notes to Chapter 2   65

3   THE CASE FOR AND AGAINST COOPERATIVE-
    COLLECTIVE PRODUCTION   66

        Notes to Chapter 3   85

4   COOPERATIVE CREDIT AND SAVINGS   86

        Africa   124
        Asia   125
        Latin America   126
        Cooperative Insurances   133
        Notes to Chapter 4   136

5   WAYS AND MEANS OF COOPERATIVE EDUCATION   138

6   COOPERATIVE AID TO DEVELOPING COUNTRIES   163

        The International Labor Conferences   164
        The Fifth Far East Agricultural
            Credit and Cooperative Workshop   170

Chapter   Page

        The International Confederation of
            Agricultural Credit   187
        The Fourth African Conference on the
            Mobilization of Local Savings   190
        The FAO Regional Seminar on
            Cooperative Farming   194
        The Second Inter-American Conference
            of Ministers of Labor   198
        The Seventh Cooperative Seminar of
            the International Cooperative
            Training Center at the University
            of Wisconsin   199
        The World Land Reform Conference   204
        The First International Conference
            on Cooperative Assistance to
            Developing Countries   205
        The First International Conference
            of the Major Cooperative Thrift
            and Credit Organizations   208
        Note to Chapter 6   209

7   COORDINATING AID TO COOPERATIVE MOVEMENTS
        IN DEVELOPING COUNTRIES   210

SELECTED BIBLIOGRAPHY   219

INDEX   227

ABOUT THE AUTHOR   239

LIST OF ABBREVIATIONS

AARRO   Afro-Asian Rural Reconstruction Organization, Addis Ababa, Ethiopia

AID   Agency for International Development,
Washington, D.C.

ASFEC   Arab States Training Center for Education
for Community Development, Sirs, Egypt

CICA   International Confederation of Agricultural
Credit, Paris, France

CUNA   Credit Union National Association (now
CUNA International), Madison, Wisconsin

FAO   Food and Agriculture Organization of the
United Nations, Rome, Italy

ICA   International Cooperative Alliance,
London, England

IFAP   International Federation of Agricultural
Producers, Washington, D.C.

IFO   Institute for Economic Research, Munich,
Germany

ILO   International Labor Office, Geneva,
Switzerland

OAS   Organization of the American States,
Washington, D.C.

OECD   Organization for Economic Cooperation and
Development, Paris, France

UNESCO   United Nations Educational, Scientific,
and Cultural Organization, Paris, France

UNICEF   United Nations Children's Emergency Fund,
            Geneva, Switzerland

WHO   World Health Organization, Geneva,
            Switzerland

Building Cooperative Movements in Developing Countries

CHAPTER **1** POLITICO-HISTORICAL AND
SOCIOECONOMIC FACTORS
IN DEVELOPING COUNTRIES

In most developing countries, historical, political, economic, and social problems are so entangled
that considering them separately is difficult, if not
unrealistic. Neither governmental motives nor regional needs can be adequately examined from only one
perspective. This is particularly true in organizing
cooperative movements. Let us briefly look at the
combined and sometimes conflicting elements of historical, political, and sociological events and situations that prevail in nearly all the areas under discussion.

The moves toward reform, modernization, and emancipation are dominated not only by the obvious needs
and wants of the emerging population, but also by the
often bewildering consequences of rash political and
ideological changes effected by leaders and the ensuing gap between them and the masses they govern.

Advisers, helpers, and researchers who come from
advanced countries to work in developing areas are,
in the beginning at least, mostly confined in their
contacts to government representatives with extremely
partisan views of their country's situation, problems,
and remedies. Also, representatives from developing
countries on visits to the United States or Europe
are, except for young trainees, usually either members
of the government or highly placed administrators.
Although they know their country and people well,
they are rarely able to make objective, candid statements on conditions and needs or to respond frankly
to questions raised by those who want to help them.

Misinterpretations and erroneous impressions resulting from introductory talks are often corrected only
if an adviser stays for a prolonged period in a foreign country and establishes contacts with well-
informed people--not always official spokesmen or
leaders. There are often contradictions between official information and the realities of a situation,
but they are rarely caused only by a deliberate dis-
tortion of facts. This is often disturbing but should
be accepted without resentment.

Leaders of developing countries are usually in a
tragic position--especially if they have seen more
advanced nations, perhaps as students at Western universities or in diplomatic or similar missions.
Aware of the shortcomings of their countrymen, they
often hide behind a mask of self-conscious pride.
This behavior gives way to a more modest and appreci-
ative manner only if the advisers and helpers react
with unfailing friendliness and patience. Confiden-
tial and friendly relationships cannot be established
until mistrust, the most serious obstacle to mutual
understanding, is overcome. This mistrust stems from
many sources, some of which can be justified--as, for
instance, suspicion of foreigners entering primitive
regions for reckless business ventures. Added sources
of mistrust are racial antagonism and the doubt
(mostly unconscious) in the minds of many leaders of
developing nations regarding their people's capacity
to fulfill the ambitious goals of their programs.

The more dominant the foreign cultural influence
prior to independence, the heavier is the weight of
insecurity and mistrust. These negative attitudes
are usually less pronounced in Asian countries where
Islam, Buddhism, Hinduism, and other ancient religions
still prevail than in African regions where, in recent times under colonial and missionary influences,
attempts have been made to supplant indigenous traditions with those of Western orientation. Because
the resulting deep resentment still exists in many
newly formed nations, they are apt to view any steps
toward modernization with suspicion.

This state of mind is closely connected with the

general reluctance of some responsible leaders to
modernize and/or educate their people in new ways and
rules visualized in their programs or political goals.
Such skeptics of Western reforms are often the most
conscientious and best representatives of their country's interests. They are aware of the dangers involved in extreme programs of modernization, such as
those undertaken in recent years in several nations
where traditions and old institutions were eliminated
by force before new ideas and methods were firmly established or understood.

Under circumstances of great urgency, immediate
action may be required regardless of such suspicions.
In such cases, the timing and methods must allow as
much as possible for the hesitancy of the people without giving up the undertaking. A decisive element in
overcoming the reluctance of governments and officials
in charge of reform work is the degree of confidence
they feel in their own positions and the amount of
support given them by the most influential groups of
their population. Seemingly dictatorial gestures
often conceal insecurity.

In contrast to reluctance and insecurity, an
eagerness to implement reforms of any kind usually
indicates that the leader believes the desired results will automatically occur once the modern techniques and methods are learned. The error of believ-
ing that tools can replace the human qualities necessary for the successful application of the tools has
often led to disappointments--a reversal of optimism
into skepticism and lack of confidence. Cooperative
establishments are especially endangered if they are
not carefully planned with due consideration of the
human factors involved. Such failures have repeatedly blocked the undertaking of new cooperative initiatives for long periods.

These negative factors should not be taken as
either a warning or a reason for pessimism with regard to the outlook for progress in developing countries. Rather, they call for additional efforts by
developed countries to promote the people's understanding of and readiness for progress. Cooperatives

are especially appropriate for overcoming such obstacles, as they tap people's inner resources. Cooperative education may counter human deficiencies
that are hard to recognize and eliminate from afar.
Close individual contacts are necessary to accomplish
what technical aid and material means alone cannot
perform.

The mental effects of the political and historical fates endured by developing nations must be recognized as fully as possible. They are often the key
to an understanding of socioeconomic phenomena: a
certain degree of resignation, opposition to progress,
negative reactions to Western values, resistance from
personalities with particularly strong feelings of
responsibility toward their countrymen. The long
colonial status of many developing countries and the
ensuing period of transition are the main sources of
many sociological and psychological barriers. Similar
conditions are found in countries with a longer history of political independence but where, until recently, the cultural and economic influences of the
West were predominant.

"Colonialism" is used by many leaders of developing countries as a convenient scapegoat to escape an
inferiority complex arising from the often unconscious
awareness of their people's backwardness. This concept, often used to blame Western civilization for the
less developed status of their former colonies, is
regarded by many leaders of emerging nations as the
primary reason for their current troubles. This tendency is particularly strong in most of the new African states but manifests itself even in countries
with more distant colonial pasts. In 1960, an Indo-
nesian leader stated that the principal weakness of
his countrymen is the ideological restraint caused by
the inhibiting effect of 300 years of colonial history. Such accusations, largely the result of Communist propaganda, are often distressing to Western
nations in their efforts to help emerging nations.
However, discussions of this theme should be avoided
by all means.

Many people in the Western world have conflicting

ideas about colonialism of the past. Some unrestrict-
edly condemn the former colonial powers and.view all
foreign aid to developing countries as overdue repa-
ration for the harm done by colonial governments.
Others point to the historical supremacy of Western
civilization and deny equal political and economic
rights to the new states. The first ask for the immediate elimination of whatever colonial or similar
ties still exist. The second see the trend toward
self-government and progress as a revolutionary assault upon the West's ancient cultural and political
primacy.

But both fail to understand the urgent demands
of today's international situation. Subjective judgments about past and present conditions are inappli-
cable to the enormous fluctuations of this century's
dynamics. The only relevant politico-historical fact
that counts is the irresistible trend of the less
fortunate sectors of humanity toward emancipation and
escape from poverty. If it wants to preserve its own
foundation, Western civilization must overcome the
problems of development. An exaggerated show of
guilt, which encourages unrealistic demands for aid,
is as wrong as high-handed gestures, which invite resistance and increased bitterness. Only by abstain-
ing from any historical criticism can the intellectual
and cultural standing of Western civilization be
demonstrated. This is the only way to refute propaganda from the Communist world and to win over those
who think of foreign aid as neo-colonialism.

Closely connected with the colonialism complex
is another major incentive to emancipation and progress: the strong nationalism of most political
leaders in the newly independent states.

The Western concept of nationalism is unknown to
most primitive populations. It had to be taught,
more or less by force, after self-government had been
achieved. Nationalism is a tragic anachronism in the
framework of present efforts toward universal recon-
ciliation. It is unfortunate that the new states embrace the concept of nineteenth-century nationalism
at a time when the Western world is beginning to hope

that two world wars are enough to convince mankind
of the dangers of extreme political nationalism.

Genuine national feelings develop where people
belong to a political unit based on common historical,
spiritual, and ethical traditions. Most developing
countries follow the opposite rule. Mixed populations
with little in common, differing in traditions, re-
ligion, and often even language, were brought under
colonial government to form pseudo-statelike communities with boundaries arbitrarily drawn by their common colonial administration, except where natural
landmarks, as in the case of islands, formed the
frontiers. After independence, these assemblages of
people and lands lacked whatever homogeneity is required for truly national units.

English, introduced in India as the official
language in the colonial era, is still indispensable
because the several hundred million people in the
country speak many different tongues and dialects.
They also represent a multitude of religious and cultural traditions. Ethnically and culturally distinct
groups live together in much smaller territories than
India. The lack of homogeneity is the historical consequence of feudal regimes, repeated conquests, migration, and other ethnic transformations, which did
not hinder the political administration of the state
as long as it was absolutist. With the universal
trend away from absolutism as well as colonialism,
these countries, like the former colonial territories,
are confronted with the same problem of bringing to
their population a consciousness of common national
feelings.

An additional obstacle is found in regions with
a partly nomadic population. Two-fifths of the 2
million inhabitants of Somalia are nomads who raise
cattle. Three-fifths are farmers, who have very little in common with the nomads. Bound together by
tribal affiliations rather than adherence to the
state, Somalian nomads often cross the frontiers to
neighboring countries, like Ethiopia and Kenya, where
they live as in Somalia. The growth of common national feelings and, even less, state consciousness is a

dubious expectation under such circumstances, at
least for the time being.

An Algerian delegate to a conference of African
leaders pointed to the great diversity in the customs,
language, and origins of his countrymen--Arabs, Ber-
bers, Mozarabs, and Kabyles. Immediately thereafter,
he mentioned Algeria's victory over French colonialism and its right to self-government, according to
tradition and origin. Thus, in order to prevent each
sector of the Algerian population from applying the
right to self-government to itself, the new government employs the triumph achieved in the struggle for
liberation to establish proud national feelings among
all of Algeria's groups.

The strong appeal to nationalism initiated by
the rulers of most newly emerged states is a calcu-
lated move to eliminate traditional loyalties along
narrower (and more genuine) lines of association.
Tribal resistance against centralized power, rival-
ries between leaders of various groups, and cultural
and religious separatism endanger national allegiance
where a natural basis does not exist. In some large
regions, nationalism fails. The establishment of the
separate states of West Pakistan, East Pakistan, and
Burma after the dissolution of British control of
India is an example of the power used by former rulers to forestall a potentially dangerous unification
of different religious and ethnic groups.

The internal struggles in the Congo and several
other African states and the unrest in many Asian
and Middle Eastern countries also illustrate the tremendous difficulties in building statelike units
where corresponding natural bonds are for the most
part nonexistent or genuine ties of tribal or regional communities have been suppressed by long periods
of colonial administration.

Moreover, the enforcement of allegiance to the
new countries is impeded by the widespread promotion
over the last decades of political self-determination
as a basic human right. This ideal has thoroughly
infiltrated colonial populations. To lead new

independent masses toward national unity when they
are disposed toward narrower associations under the
right of self-determination is possible only if national feelings supersede the old ideas. This explains why most new governments attempt to revive
memories of former periods of glory, of long-forgotten
myths and legends, of heroic deeds performed by ancestors in an effort to evoke pride in belonging to
an old (even if forgotten) national body.

The politics of stimulating national feelings is
the first step toward consolidating and organizing
cultural and economic developments. Cooperatives,
in particular, often succeed if they are thought of
as a national duty, the same as land reforms and cultivation of new territories. In Egypt, for instance,
the patriotic enthusiasm of former slave workers, recently settled in agricultural cooperatives in the
"Liberation Province," provides dramatic evidence of
the eventual usefulness of national inspiration, provided that it does not lead to superstition, hostility
toward foreigners, and similar exaggerations.

In newly formed nations, all the leaders and
large sectors of the populations are obsessed with
the idea of having been, and still being, exploited.
Economic and other exploitation, which is inherent in
all primitive societies, has grown into a decisive
element of political propaganda in both internal and
external affairs. No government can ignore the extreme examples of exploitation by feudal classes, by
native merchants, and by usurers, found in most developing countries. These abuses must be abolished
as completely as the "imperialistic exploitation" by
former colonial powers and the "misdeeds" of foreign
merchants who in some regions have monopolized export
and import activities. The evident phenomenon of
exploitation, whether from natives or foreigners, is
used to excuse many actual causes of primitiveness
and to protect well-informed national leaders from
self-reproach.

Protests from foreigners against the one-sided
and exaggerated excuse of exploitation as the cause
of all deprivations are meaningless and can only

shake the already-weak self-confidence of many
leaders.

The challenge to stop exploitation is a strong
motivation for opening cooperative establishments.
Their promoters point to the historical fact that the
exploitation of economically weak individuals by the
ruthless power of superior forces has led to the success of the cooperative movement in the Western world.

Most institutions established in colonial times
are now accused of being mere tools of exploitation,
regardless of their genuine social purposes. If they
are still maintained by the new governments, their
colonial origin is often denied or they are reorganized in a way that makes exploitation impossible.
Examples are the British preparatory schools for natives entering public service in India, and the
Sociétés de Prévoyance (Societies of Provident Care)
in the former French and Belgian colonies of Africa.

The enduring association of the cooperative establishments in Nigeria with British cooperative organizations represents a remarkable exception to the
widespread animosity elsewhere against colonial institutions. Director W. Waidelich of the German
cooperative school in Stuttgart-Hohenheim points to
the lasting benefits of close ties between the Nigerian cooperatives and sponsoring organizations in
England. A Nigerian cooperative law was established
under British administration as early as 1936 and
has since been unchanged.

The Sociétés de Prévoyance were established
mainly in the first years of this century. They have
created a legacy of resentment that illustrates the
often unqualified aversion toward past colonial institutions. Just mentioning their names to representatives of succeeding governments generates a bitter
response.

The primary objective of the Sociétés was to
collect food reserves for scarce times and to provide
facilities for transportation and storage. A broader
goal was to educate people in the need for precautions

in their daily work. Despite this well-intentioned
program, which present leaders admit to be in line
with their goal of instilling prudent and cooperative
activities, the Sociétés are now regarded as symbols
of colonial exploitation and as the main source of
their people's mistrust of all the efforts to establish organizations with similar programs, including
cooperative societies. This paradox is the result of
two administrative factors:

1) Compulsory membership of all landowners and
enforced contributions, imposed and collected like
taxes.

2) Exclusion of natives from any administrative
function.

Thus, the members had no control of either the
management or the use made of the considerable amounts
of money collected, which, according to the Sociétés'
statutes, were to be spent for the benefit of the
contributors only.

Whether these Sociétés could have been made viable without legal enforcement is an open question.
The same is true of the matter of whether natives
could have taken over administrative and controlling
functions. Nonetheless, the two regulations were
serious psychological blunders by the colonial administration.

While the work of the Sociétés was certainly not
without fault, it is hard to believe that corruption
and mismanagement could have been so appalling as to
justify the present accusations. The fact that valuable equipment and considerable funds were left
when the native administrations took over the Sociétés
testifies to the contrary. But quotations from African leaders[1] reflect their resentment, regardless of
what actually happened.

Niger: "After reaching autonomy, the rural population generally asked for the liquidation of the
Sociétés de Prévoyance, established in 1919, because
the enforced transfer of reserve stocks to the

Sociétés was not regarded as an act of self-help. In addition, political discrimination was widespread because of the exclusion of natives from the Sociétés' administration."

Ivory Coast: "The general mistrust of governmental aid, specifically the application of cooperative methods, is based on the experience with the administration of the former Sociétés de Prévoyance, the leaders of which were men capable of everything and good for nothing."

Guinea: "The unique purpose of the Sociétés de Prévoyance was to collect money without any regard for the farmers' interests. The consequent mistrust prevented until 1957 the majority of the Parliament from consenting to any encouragement of cooperative work by the state."

Dahomey: "The Sociétés de Prévoyance were established in 1929 under a French decree of 1910, and were administered by government officials exclusively; the officials' false allocation of funds nourished the suspicion of corruption."

Mali: "The Sociétés de Prévoyance, established after 1919, and the institution of cooperative organizations under the colonial regime were complete failures. They were to the benefit of a small upper-class group only and were designed to facilitate colonial domination."

Togo: "The development of a cooperative movement was inhibited from 1934 until 1957 because of the actions taken by the Sociétés de Prévoyance. In spite of their programs, seemingly in line with agricultural needs, their bureaucratism provoked resistance and paralyzed private initiative."

These critical remarks illustrate the fact that, in the minds of most Africans, the Sociétés are the embodiment of "colonial exploitation." This conviction is a major reason for opposition to new programs with similar goals, such as cooperatives.

This leads to the conclusion that proper administrative methods are as relevant as sound programs and goals in establishing institutions to help less developed people help themselves. The discredit into which the Sociétés de Prévoyance have fallen should be taken as a lesson to avoid as far as possible even the appearance of enforcement and compulsion in new cooperatives.

However, most of those who work in aid to developing countries admit that governmental initiative and directives are indispensable. Fully voluntary membership and participation in such organizations can hardly be expected in the foreseeable future. Thus, careful planning for education in self-administration is extremely important and should, from the outset, form an integral part of the preparatory work of cooperatives.

In Niger and Congo-Brazzaville, for instance, there are still compulsory deliveries of agricultural products to various government agencies and obligations to build up reserve stocks. In some districts, the former Sociétés continue under changed names, such as "Sociétés Mutuelles de Production Rurale" (Mutual Societies of Rural Production). According to a report from Dahomey, the much criticized enforced contributions are still required in many regions of the country, and the former Sociétés' practice of transferring part of the collections to a distant center of administration continues. A governmental Bank of Development collects these sums to build up "guarantee funds" for investment credit to be granted to cooperative societies. Under colonial administration, a similar practice led to the charge that the money was spent for administrative purposes instead of help to the contributing farmers. In reality, it was deposited in reserve funds to cover eventual local deficits where credits were not collectable.

Right or wrong, in institutions established by the colonial governments, there is at least a possibility of misuse of power when goals are not met. With much less logic, however, internal exploitation is often charged to colonial powers. They are censured by some of the new leaders for not having put an end to usury, feudalism, and commercial monopolism. They are accused of willfully using the internal forces of exploitation as tools for the enslavement of the masses. In most cases, this is mere demagogy, and an intelligent leader would never believe this kind of propaganda. He knows full well that exploitation by internal groups has been one of the earliest and most serious causes of social and economic restraints.

On a worldwide basis, free trade has always been blamed for exploiting the weakness of farmers, artisans, small businessmen, and poor consumers--a situation that has generated the initial impulse to establish cooperative organizations. The lack of trade experience, the inability to reach the appropriate markets, the producers' shortage of monetary resources--these and many other deficiencies that exist in the early stages of economic development make the help of intermediaries essential. Well aware that they are indispensable, they reward themselves unscrupulously. The disastrous terms on which credits are granted, the consequences of farmers' selling their products at tremendous sacrifices, and the resulting loss of land and home are primary reasons for the accumulation of land by non-farmers and for the masses of formerly independent but now slave laborers.

In many areas, religious and/or traditional practices contribute to the impoverishment of landowners by the division of property among heirs. The result is economically unworkable units that increase the new owners' dependence on traders and other intermediaries who finally dispossess them. Also, the land splitting adds to the traditional power of feudal landlords and increases their social prerogatives. These often are backed by religious leaders, regardless of the retarding influences on social progress.

The predominantly agrarian character of most developing nations, together with their supply of certain raw materials of high value to industrialized countries, makes the export of these materials necessary to pay for the import of required goods. Export

and import activities were almost exclusively controlled by free traders--foreigners or natives--who
monopolized these lifelines of producers and consumers. Farmers and artisans became mere pawns in the
transactions on which their existence depended--
another cause of exploitation inherent in the very
nature of the economic structure.

An exception is seen in Greece, where continuous political disturbances have, over nearly a century, hampered economic and social progress without
eliminating the indigenous commercial talents of the
Greek people. As soon as the wars and revolutions
of recent years ended, cooperative self-help started
again to revive the export and import trade. A
visitor to Greek cooperatives was, until recently,
confronted with a remarkable contrast between the
local cooperative societies and the central cooperative organizations in charge of collecting, processing, and shipping export goods. The former were still
in the initial stages of development, while the latter, under the leadership of the Panhellenic Confederation of Agricultural Cooperatives--the center of
more than a dozen unions, each with between 50- and
120-member societies--were an efficient tool of Greek
foreign trade.

Except for Greece, the impression prevails that
the foreign trade of most developing countries is a
vital basis of their existence, and, at the same time,
one of the main areas of exploitation for free traders. From this situation stems a general animosity
against aliens, not only where Western powers dominate foreign trade but also, to no lesser degree, in
some East African and South Asian regions, including
India, where a large share of export and import
transactions has long been controlled by the Chinese.

In Burma, where communications with the outside
world were scarce until the second half of the nineteenth century, mistrust and criticism of foreign
influences are still found. This mistrust is directed even at developments of indisputable progress.
In 1960, a Burmese delegate to the first International
Cooperative Seminar of the German Foundation for the

Developing Countries described the idyllic conditions
under which Burmese farmers had lived in the independent Kingdom of Burma, when agricultural indebtedness
was unknown. After Burma's incorporation into the
British Empire, indebtedness came into being as a consequence of colonial land-ownership regulations.
These new rules, which were no doubt beneficial, established free ownership to the first cultivators of
land after twelve years of uninterrupted cultivation;
during this time, the farmers were free to dispose
of their products. According to the delegate, this
formerly unknown institution of land ownership for
those who created new cultivations led to agricultural indebtedness by giving usurers their first opportunity to mortgage the newly acquired lots and impos-
ing unbearable conditions upon the farmers.

A second disturbing factor, according to the
Burmese delegate, was the opening of the Suez Canal
in 1869 (also the approximate date of the establishment of the land ownership mentioned above). The
Canal opened new means for exporting rice, Burma's
main product, and so provided new opportunities for
"foreign speculation." Additional loans were granted
to the farmers so they could extend their rice plan-
tations and meet the increasing export demands. Thus,
the delegate disregarded the positive aspects of the
new land ownership and stressed only the negative
ones: indebtedness, loss of land, and the rise of a
new class of agrarian proletarians that is now one
of the government's most serious concerns. It would
have been hopeless to try to change the delegate's
mind by raising questions about the farmers' living
standard during the golden age of the Kingdom, when
peasants were debtless because they did not own any
land on which to borrow.

This illustrates how Asian and African leaders
look for scapegoats outside their own spheres of
responsibility--scapegoats that can explain the primitiveness of their countrymen in terms of "imported"
reforms and subsequent exploitation.

Similar attitudes were reflected in a report
from India. The native private traders were, it was

said, never reckless as long as the self-governing
bodies in the Indian villages were in existence.
Under these, no trader dared to disregard his obligation to be fair to the village community. Only
after dispersion of the village-controlled order by
the British colonial government did the traders start
to communicate with others in urban centers about
trading and moneylending operations, and they were
thus led to disregard the villagers' interests. This
exploitation by native merchants and usurers was thus
a direct result of colonial regulations.

It is useless to debate the historical truth of
these attempts to blame colonialism for all current
problems. These charges cannot be criticized by
foreigners without seriously impairing the harmony
required for successful common efforts toward progress. Both the Burmese and the Indian delegate firmly
believed in their governments' reform programs and
were sincerely trying to promote understanding at the
seminar by pointing out the specific problems at home
without injuring their countries' reputation. Colonialism makes a convenient scapegoat.

The oldest element of exploitation and the
greatest obstacles to progress in developing countries
is the feudalistic social structure. The strength
of feudalism varies. Some Mediterranean, South Asian,
and South American regions suffer much more from feudal domination than most sub-Saharan African countries.
In the latter, tribal mores dictate land ownership
and distribution in ways that resemble traditional
feudal patterns. Rarely, however, do these lead to
an exploitation of the lower classes comparable to
that in countries where the feudal owners of large
estates and/or powerful groups of capitalists (a
more modern version of feudalism) suppress the
poverty-stricken majority of the population. The
governments resent some remaining tribal privileges
more than the people, because they often obstruct
agrarian and social reforms.

Even in countries where traditional feudalism
seemingly has been overcome by successful revolution,
its power is still felt--for example, in a country

adjacent to another with a hitherto-unrestricted feudal system. This contrast exists in some regions of the Middle East and is responsible for the slow pace of social and, specifically, agrarian reforms.

Mustapha Kemal (Ataturk), the leader of the Turkish revolution of 1923 and thereafter the first President of the Turkish Republic, was an ardent social reformer. During the fifteen years of his leadership, he applied all his energies to eliminating feudalism. However, soon after his death in 1938, it became evident that the decade and a half of his anti-feudal drive was not sufficient to overcome the reactionary forces in Turkey. Despite legislative, educational, and other efforts to improve the peasants' standard of living, including the establishment of agricultural cooperatives, the obstructive influence of large estate owners, who had regained political power, became obvious soon after Ataturk's death. With the help of religious leaders, whose negative influence on education had been one of the President's many concerns, the Turkish reactionaries succeeded in making the peasants suspicious of agrarian reforms in general, even when their need was realized.

To this writer, who lived in Turkey during the last years of progress under Ataturk's leadership as well as for some years afterwards, this was a dramatic example of the dangers involved in pushing reforms beyond the capacity of large parts of the population and contrary to traditional powers. Overzealousness merely strengthens the reactionary forces.

As long as only a small elite understands the ideas behind social-reform programs, no matter how carefully planned and well-intentioned, failures are unavoidable. And every such failure becomes a weapon in the hands of reactionary forces, mainly where they still exercise the political and economic power of large-estate ownership and other wealth.

In contrast to the Turkish example, the revolution in Egypt resulted in an immediate assault upon feudal traditionalism. Unlike the Turkish revolution, which was part of the general upheaval following

World War I, the Egyptian revolt was deliberately
planned in peace to bring freedom to the suppressed
masses. There was, furthermore, much more readiness
for reform in the Egypt of 1952 than in the Turkey of
1923. The nearly thirty years between the outbreak of
the two revolutions had spread progressive ideas all
over the world and prepared at least fragments of most
developing populations for radical changes.

Thus, President Nasser received immediate support from large groups of enthusiastic followers,
mainly well-educated members of the Egyptian middle-
class--a group that during Ataturk's revolution had
very little influence in Turkey. Where Ataturk ex-
hausted himself by personally teaching and introducing the new ideas and methods of government, work,
and daily life into the cities and villages of his
country with the assistance of only a handful of followers, Nasser from the beginning had the advantage
of being able to place comparatively large segments
of the reform work into the hands of trustworthy,
well-trained men.

A few months after he came to power, Nasser succeeded in breaking up the largest estates by legal
action. As amended in 1961, the law limited private
land holdings to approximately fifty hectares. Similarly, he abolished certain feudal prerogatives in
the non-agrarian sectors of the country's economic
structure. In the opinion of Egypt's present leaders, feudal exploitation is a much greater cause of
poverty than the influence of foreigners during the
second half of the nineteenth century. The term
"cooperative" stands next to the adjectives "democratic" and "socialistic" in Egypt's new constitution,
characterizing the principles on which government
and public life shall be based.

The Egyptian opposition to feudalism causes certain conflicts between the internal socialistic and
the external nationalistic concepts of the government.
The latter, which are expressed in Nasser's pan-Arab
program, are complicated by typical Arab feudalism,
which still prevails in most neighboring states. This
conflict is felt by many Egyptians, who often give

foreigners the impression that the role of social progress will depend on whether emphasis is laid on pan-Arabism or on internal social reforms. It is fortunate that the great majority of the agrarian population, which feels the immediate effects of social and specifically cooperative efforts, is apparently more interested in social progress than in foreign policies.

Iran's drive against feudalism is characterized by the ruler's personal initiative. In 1951, the Shah decided to transfer a region comprising more than 2,000 villages from royal to public ownership. A special law promulgating this act was enacted in 1956. Prior to this, more than a quarter of the land in Iran was privately owned by men who possessed territories the size of whole provinces. At that time, 20 to 25 per cent of the land was cultivable, but only between 10 and 15 per cent was being plowed. By a law passed in 1959, individually owned property was not to exceed 400 hectares of irrigatable land and 800 hectares of non-cultivable territory. Soon after 1959, the Shah established and financed a Development Bank which works to promote the establishment of cooperative societies. But even the most enthusiastic supporters of these reforms admit that the Shah's program encounters strong opposition from feudal interests. They fight his efforts to settle large numbers of peasants on their own farms and to reduce Iran's nomadism, which is one of the greatest obstacles to agrarian reform. The Shah's adversaries are said to exploit conflicts in foreign policy and to be behind the recurring Kurdish insurrections, which are among the gravest disturbances to Iran's stability. This illustrates the determination of the proponents of feudalism to defend their status--even against the highest authorities. The leading officials of the Shah's reform institutions believe that feudalism will ultimately be defeated. Among them are members of formerly dominant families, who are evidence of the fact that many Iranian aristocrats, mainly in the younger generation, are not opposed to social reforms.

Iran is not the only nation experiencing a

diminishing opposition to social improvements from
people who until recently did not want social progress. Their motives may not always be altruistic.
The most adamant reactionaries cannot fail to see
the increasing poverty among the rapidly growing populations of most developing countries and the consequent danger of Communism. But whatever their motives, the fact remains that social-consciousness is
growing among formerly reactionary classes in many
regions. Reports from Latin America, for instance,
indicate some remarkable progress. In different
parts of the world, the promotion of cooperative
methods in agriculture and other areas is receiving
increasing support from former feudal and industrial
leaders.

It may appear over-optimistic to count these
hopeful but still scarce symptoms of fading prejudices
as active socioeconomic incentives to progress in
developing countries. But unprejudiced advisers will
always find persons in all classes and groups of the
population whose appreciation of and devotion to the
social-reform work performed in their country will
outweigh other disappointments and resistance.

One more negative factor must be discussed. This
is the suspicion, which every Westerner must be prepared to encounter, that the intentions of some of
the more advanced nations are basically dishonest.
This feeling is often substantiated by pointing to
the extended aid given to certain dictatorial governments in the Middle East and in Latin America in
the recent past. Undoubtedly, there are examples of
aid to developing countries that was undertaken primarily to offset Communism and without due care to
properly allocate the grants to programs of social
progress. However, they do not justify a general
suspicion of deliberate help to the forces of social
regression. The mechanics and organization of aid
are tremendously complex and difficult. Great care
must be taken to ensure that the funds go in the right
way, at the right time, to the right authorities.

The necessary education and training of persons
to allocate the urgently requested funds had not been

accomplished yet, when, in the late forties and early fifties, Western governments were deluged by requests for immediate help. There was often no way to adequately investigate the demands for help, which seemed to be urgent in order to prevent a total breakdown of the existing order, thus creating a dangerous void. Painstakingly organized and well-functioning institutions for foreign aid to developing countries are, in most developed nations, the result of long years of hard work, trial and error, diligent research, and careful education of many diverse specialists. Moreover, considerable efforts were required within most Western nations to convince governments and influential groups of the urgency for help and to appropriate the immense human and monetary means that were needed. These efforts are rarely understood by leaders of countries where Western-style democracy is practically unknown. The suspicion of dishonest motives behind the aid to developing countries is, to a large degree, nourished, if not initiated, by Communist propaganda, which created the slogans of "neo-colonialism" and "neo-imperialism."

Where developed countries expect adverse criticism, it is advisable for them not to proclaim too loudly the self-evident social and democratic purposes of an aid program. Only results can overcome doubt and suspicion. This approach is particularly true in cooperative work, where the principles and methods, as practiced in the West, may need considerable modification to suit conditions in most developing countries. The primary aims and goals of new governmental cooperative programs often require the Westerners to do much adapting of their ideas and concepts, especially in comprehending the paradox to which leaders of most developing nations are committed--the dictating of democracy.

NOTE TO CHAPTER 1

1. These statements were part of the reports of African leaders to a cooperative seminar of the German Foundation for Developing Countries held in Berlin-Tegel in the summer of 1962. Translated from the original French by the author.

CHAPTER **2** MOTIVATIONS, GOALS,
AND OBSTACLES FOR
COOPERATIVE
ESTABLISHMENTS

In view of the multitude, variety, and inter-
relatedness of the problems encountered in developing
countries, it is almost impossible to establish general rules for organizing cooperative movements. The
inevitable gap between principles and rules and the
practical decisions to be made in individual cases
accounts for the wide diversity of opinion on cooperative methods as an appropriate means of progress.
Western advisers are particularly doubtful about cooperative programs that deviate from traditional concepts and/or exceed the limits of genuine cooperative
conditions, whereas leaders of developing countries
often have much looser and vaguer ideas of what cooperatives should do.

Apparently this problem was in the mind of the
former president of the International Cooperative
Alliance, W. P. Watkins, when he addressed a conference of cooperators from Middle Eastern and Asian
countries in 1960. He pointed to the difference between "Cooperation with a capital C" and "cooperation
with a small c." He defined the first as a movement
that ties its members together by their common will
to combine individual forces in one enterprise, to
develop a self-sustaining body, and so to promote the
community's economic, social, and individual standards.
He explained "cooperation with a small c" as any kind
of working together toward specific restricted purposes, such as supply of material or sale of products,
merely as a matter of business interests. In many
cases, this represents considerable progress. For
many people in poor countries where exploitation by

traders has been the rule, the replacement of mistrust and mutual deceit by decent methods of bargain-
ing may appear to be such an accomplishment that they
may believe that they have reached the status of
"good cooperators." The absence of regular cooperative ties and forms in many such institutions pre-
vents the establishment of a genuine cooperative
spirit and the formation of elements of educational
and cultural impact on the whole community. Mr.
Watkins' admonition was directed toward the lack of
essential prerequisites of cooperation in its true
sense, which so often is found in the initial stages
of cooperation in developing countries.

A loose definition of the term "cooperation"
appears in the new Egyptian constitution, which contains the adjective "cooperative" as one of the three
characteristic principles of the administration. This
may explain in some measure why organizations established primarily to promote and to perform governmental programs are often called "cooperatives" without
(or at least prior to) fulfilling the structural and
other requirements of genuine cooperation.

Similar conditions exist in parts of India, in
the Congo, and in other African countries. They are
drastically expressed in a report, issued in Cairo,
of the address by a long-term leader of the agricultural cooperative movement in Egypt, Mahmud Fawzy, to
a technical conference on "Cooperatives in the Near
East." The introductory paragraph illustrates cooperative ideas in Egypt.

> At the present time, the agricultural coop-
> erative societies in the Egyptian region
> are not mere institutions to serve its mem-
> bers or cooperative shops to sell fertili-
> zers and seeds . . . at reduced prices.
> During the past recent years, the system
> of cooperation has radically developed. Its
> role grew more positive. Apart from the
> services the cooperatives extend to the
> members, they became today the means and
> channel to implement the economic and social
> policy of the state.[1]

This tendency is a natural consequence of governmental initiatives in cooperative ventures and is a problem encountered repeatedly. The author believes that governmental initiative and aid in building cooperative movements is an indispensable instrument of progress in most developing countries--at least for the time being and the near future. It would be unrealistic to ignore the fact that government-sponsored cooperatives are bound to become tools for implementing state policies. But this is not necessarily incompatible with cooperative goals so long as the policies are not contrary to the final objectives of cooperation in the economic field in which they are applied. If combined with educational efforts toward future self-administration and independence, the cooperative initiative by governments of developing countries should not be criticized in the light of orthodox Western theories. The educational factor is a decisive criterion of a government's ultimate cooperative inclinations. Where appropriate educational steps do not accompany the formation of cooperative institutions from the very start, it is doubtful whether they can later free themselves from governmental influence. The "cooperatives" in most Communist countries are an extreme example of how the cooperative form can be misused to undermine private ownership, destroy individual action, and suppress the basic principle of cooperation under democratic administration.

The future course of many new governments is still uncertain. Education toward self-help and self-administratiion in the framework of cooperative principles helps to prevent destructive turns.

An indeterminate form of state socialism characterizes the politico-economic systems of most developing countries, thus making governmental directives and controls unavoidable. This is true even where the initiative to develop cooperative establishments comes from the private sector. However, the expectation is justified, and in various countries already realized, that cooperatives can eventually attain their objectives of self-administration and independence even when their modest beginnings under governmental control are contrary to these principles.

Socioeconomic objectives and political aims appear to be intermingled in various forms. In India, for instance, cooperative programs and motives show considerable variation throughout different regions of the country's vast territory. These variations are conditioned by the different relationships between the central government and the cooperative leadership of the individual Indian states or provinces. Two Indian delegates to a 1960 seminar sponsored by the German Institute for the Developing Countries discussed their beliefs as to the future trends in Indian agricultural cooperation. The first delegate, a leader of a large group of cooperatives, had rebuilt the cooperative organization, which, he said, had lost its significance because of the colonial regime's destructive effects on the farmers' "genuine cooperative spirit." He emphasized the necessity of requiring cooperative education in all village elementary schools, taking due consideration of the socialistic aspects of the central Indian Government but focusing primarily on the particular conditions prevailing in the village or region.

The second report was given by a young government official, a "registrar"--government representative in charge of surveying the condition and development of cooperative societies. He felt that existing regional and other individual tendencies, which he called "exaggerated individualism," should be eliminated as they were the main cause of the still-prevailing "stagnant village life" in India. Only a centrally administered program--including education-- could transform cooperation into a national movement, he observed. The goal of "forming the farmers' spirit and future" could never be accomplished unless cooperation was made an "affair of state."

At the same seminar, a representative of Thailand stressed the need for governmental leadership in promoting cooperation by pointing to the peasant's indifference to improvements; this attitude, he declared, was the government's main concern. During the past forty years of cooperative efforts in Thailand, only

8 per cent of the agrarian population had joined the
movement, although 90 per cent of the cultivable land
was in the hands of small and needy farmers. They
were usually uninterested in expansion and improvement, and preferred the traditional ways of producing
only for the family. They were indifferent to the
national economy and to contacts with the market. To
overcome these deficiencies, the government organized
a cooperative credit system in 1959. The system re-
placed land values as criteria of credit with individual productivity standards. This was combined
with a program of "work education," performed by cooperative methods of credit survey. A new phase of
the hitherto stagnant cooperative movement seemed to
be in view and justifies the government's initiative.

A report from Niger, presented to a second seminar of the German Institute in 1962, again pointed
to the government's obligation to promote cooperation
for educational purposes. The "generally stagnant"
life in the rural areas of Niger was said to be primarily responsible for the "embryonic" state of that
country's economy, a condition that only administrative initiative could overcome. The report primarily
blamed the former colonial administration for the
poor conditions, and characterized the government's
efforts to abolish them as "re-education of the youth
to the traditional honesty of the country's history"
and as "reinstatement of the old village communities,
destroyed by the colonial administration." The report clearly indicated, however, that before cooperative or any other organizational work could succeed,
some basic problems, aside from those caused by the
ever-present colonial residue, must be solved.

A large part of Niger's population is nomads;
getting them permanently settled would be a step toward filling the large uninhabited distances between
villages. This is essential, as the country's political, social, and economic future depends upon the
growth of a system of nonisolated human settlements.
The government of Niger plans to organize the projected settlements in cooperative form, thereby also
solving the problems of "re-education." This plan
illustrates the faith in the powers of cooperation

held by formerly subdued people, who believe that
liberty automatically gives them the capacity and
knowledge required for self-administration. Enthusiastic leaders with these convictions are, of course,
the most valuable elements of the newly emerging societies, but they tend to disregard the necessity for
careful planning and step-by-step implementation of
it. It is often difficult to make them realize that
caution must be applied for cooperative establishments to succeed.

Under such circumstances, it is highly important
to grant aid to cooperative projects only on the basis of preparatory studies of their motivations and
goals. In 1961, the Special Advisory Committee on
Cooperatives of the Agency for International Development (AID) issued a memorandum, "Cooperatives Democratic Institutions for Economic and Social Development," outlining certain principles to be strictly
observed in order to prevent the waste of funds and
efforts. The main prerequisites of effective assistance are stated in six recommendations. The first
deals with studies of the "Feasibility and Adaptability of the Cooperative Program," i.e., finding out
what specific needs exist and are recognized by the
respective sectors of the population. The other recommendations refer to investigations of the conform-
ity to the cultural, traditional, and mental status
of the people involved, to the assignment of specialists in the respective fields to perform corresponding "feasibility studies," to set aside in every
project's budget the amounts required for such preparatory work, and to reserve up to two months for
the studies before deciding upon what aid should be
granted to the project.

Although the recommended feasibility studies are
costly and time-consuming, they may prevent the loss
of much more money and time on utopian and illusory
projects initiated without preparation. Moreover,
experience has repeatedly shown that whenever a project fails, cooperative work in general is discredited
and cannot be reinstated for considerable time. Fortunately, the realities of work actually in progress
often reveal the unattainability of vague and

exaggerated goals. In the absence of detailed feasibility studies, the original plan can sometimes be adjusted in the initial stages of the work, when immediate requirements overshadow unrealistic final objectives.

Some progress reports from Egypt and Iran illustrate this juxtaposition of current work and final objectives. Where a program embraces several objectives, such as cultivation of new land, land distribution, settlement of landless people, and soil improvement, priorities must be given to particular actions that sometimes alter or set back the original schedule in favor of positive, if limited results. Under such circumstances, conflicts between planning officials, who usually do not live on location, and those responsible for the actual progress of the work can hardly be avoided. Some reports reflect the impatience of ambitious officials when programs are discontinued or time schedules are altered. The unpleasant role of intermediary between planners and performers often has to be assumed by the foreign adviser or expert for the disputed project. This requires great tact and a clear understanding of the factual, personal, and sometimes political implications of the project. In order to prevent visiting inspectors from giving unnecessary critical reports to their superiors, the expert has to know all the facts favoring the required changes, the advantages of partial solutions, the value of what already has been done, and the danger of adhering to original plans that are clearly impractical. Where cooperative work is involved, a demonstration of the first signs of solidarity among the new members, and of their beginning to understand the meaning and goals of cooperation, may do more to convince critical outsiders of the necessity to carry on the initial work without undue pressure than more tangible facts about the scheduled program.

The experience of many American and European experts demonstrates that in nearly every project of greater significance technical, social, and political motivations combine to form an ambitious program exceeding the immediate objectives of cooperative work.

This is particularly true in countries where the masses were promised a "golden age" after liberation from "colonial suppression."

The new leaders often admit that they follow a two-edged cooperative policy by granting the promised help only to those who join the ad hoc established "cooperative societies." The benefit of settlement projects, structural adjustments, and improvement of their lots, irrigation, and other installations for ameliorating agricultural work are shared by "members of cooperatives" only. Thus, the large membership of new cooperatives in many developing countries far exceeds that attainable through the principle of voluntarism in Western cooperative movements. This "enforced membership"--which, of course, is never expressed in any cooperative law--throws a dubious light on many of the new units.

The practice of attracting new members by excluding nonmembers from state-granted privileges is also used in establishing credit facilities; no sources of loans at reasonable terms exist except for funds provided by the government. In Egypt, for instance, public credit is channeled exclusively through cooperative banks in order to demonstrate the government's successful program of cooperation.

But to insist upon voluntary membership would mean to abstain from building cooperatives in developing countries. Most leaders of the new movements are well aware of the weakness of their membership policies. They offer convincing reasoning for not rigidly applying the principle of voluntarism in the initial stages of cooperative work. To get the people "under control," they say, is their paramount goal. They are generally confident that, by granting financial and other help by means of cooperative association, the framework for building the social and educational prerequisites of cooperation in more or less enforced bodies will come into being in a manner that guarantees lasting effects. As long as an educational program accompanies the organizational and technical instruction of the new members from the beginning, they contend, no objection can be justified.

In Egypt, India, Greece, and other developing
countries, where there are special training courses
for members, officers, inspectors, and others, a
broad base will soon be established from which instruction may be spread over all parts of the organization. The outcome is more doubtful in new cooperative units that leave education to later stages.

Governmental influence on cooperative movements
in developing countries seems to be an unending topic
of discussion, and has been the subject of numerous
reports and publications in recent years. But after
more than two decades of many Western experts' experience in cooperative work in new communities, there
should no longer be any doubt that government initiative, assistance, and control is a condition sine qua
non of building cooperative movements, and that the
media are at hand or can always be mobilized to avoid
permanent state control. An especially significant
commentary was made by one of the most experienced
leaders in this field, John M. Eklund, who in 1963
reported on his observations in seven Asian and two
African countries that he had visited as project director of the combined development program of the
National Farmers Union and AID. In his report, he
stated:

> In every instance, the cooperative movement
> is being built from the government outward,
> with an extension of government in manage-
> ment, direction, planning, and operation.
> Such procedures appear absolutely essential
> at the present but do present a critical
> problem for the future in the development
> of an independent cooperative movement.

Later in the report, he observed about West Pakistan:

> Again, as in East Pakistan and in Cambodia,
> the will to move by government in a coopera-
> tive fashion is firm and fixed, but the great
> gap in know-how and understanding by members
> leaves the program almost entirely to gov-
> ernment impetus and planning. Without a
> training program of managers selected by the

cooperatives and a program of information
and understanding of the purpose of cooperation, it will remain a government-
dominated enterprise and eventually lead
to the nationalization of agriculture,
agricultural marketing, and processing.

Mr. Eklund also met with leaders of the National
Cooperative Marketing Association in New Delhi, an
organization he describes as having been formed "independent of government . . . attempting to develop
marketing cooperatives and assist these with credit
through a cooperative bank also organized indepen-
dently. The comments of these men suggested that a
government-oriented cooperative movement would eventually defeat the basic purposes of cooperation."

These few remarks, which resemble comments in
reports by other knowledgeable people, sufficiently
characterize the generally prevailing government-
cooperative relationship. The dangers are noted,
but also the fact that these dangers are clearly seen
both inside and outside the movements, and steps to
protect the delicate balance are being undertaken or
at least considered.

The main safeguard is education of members, employees, and--last but not least--the whole population of the village or region. A frequently voiced
objection is that it is difficult to bring cooperative education to the least civilized areas, but this
is not true. A striking example is the successful
work of CUNA (formerly Credit Union National Association) International agents in the poorest and least
developed regions of Latin America and other areas.
Often, district authorities were surprised at the
fast results achieved when people with no knowledge
of such matters were brought together into small
groups of savings and loan associations.

This success depends on the ability and zeal of
somebody living among the people who understands
their individual needs and knows how to gain their
confidence. The first such pioneer work was performed
by various Roman Catholic priests in different parts

of South America. In later periods, CUNA International worked (and still works) with members of the
Peace Corps, who are trained in all aspects of education for cooperative work, in credit-union programs
and methods, and in local sociological and economic
conditions. The CUNA method of education for thrift
has grown into a basic element of initial cooperative
training. It is easily understood by the most primitive people, to whom the smallest accumulation of
savings is evidence of the material and moral value
of cooperative saving.

Leaders of development programs who neglect this
paramount factor of education and promotion are ques-
tionable advocates of self-help institutions, regardless of what they proclaim to the contrary. Their
favorite objection--that people are still too poor to
save any money--is insignificant, as evidenced by
numerous successes achieved under highly adverse conditions. Objections to early savings promotions often reflect a fear that fast accumulations of savings
may bring financial independence too soon and thus
block continuous government influence and control.

The following story, which this writer likes to
tell whenever he meets people skeptical of savings
promotion, was originally told by an East Asian leader
of agricultural cooperatives to a number of colleagues
from neighboring countries after a lecture on
cooperative-financing problems at the 1960 seminar in
Berlin. After three or four participants had expressed doubts about savings campaigns in their districts, the leader told of an experiment in one of
the poorest regions of his country. The rice planters
there had produced only enough rice to meet their
private needs. A cooperative society was established
with a modest government loan, and the planters were
invited to become members. Their only initial obligation was to set aside, in a small sack provided by
the society, one spoonful of rice per member of the
family at each meal. The society collected the sacks
at regular intervals and credited the members for the
quantity and quality of rice in each sack. After a
time, a small tool or implement was sent back to each
member along with the empty sack and the explanation

that this was equivalent to part of the credit in
their accounts. This practice was quickly and easily
understood, and not only demonstrated the value of
savings but also stimulated production. The planters
learned to understand the supply and market functions
of a cooperative. Later, they were supplied with
fertilizers, insecticides, and other valuable commodities and taught how to use them and improve their
general level of production. In less than three years,
the cooperative grew into a well-functioning, multipurpose society that had begun to amortize the initial
government loan.

The success of any experiment of this kind depends on laying the proper foundation in small districts. It is equally important that the initiative
of local leaders, who are familiar with the specific
conditions in the district, not be hampered by government agents or central authorities so long as their
actions serve the general objectives of the cooperative program. The administrative machinery of many
developing countries is still uncertain, and frequent
organizational modifications affecting both personnel
and administrative functions hinder local progress.
It seems to be inevitable in newly formed (or ascend-
ing) administrations that responsibility is frequently
shifted from one department to another, and that competition between individual departments, particularism, and bureaucratism--mainly on the lower echelons--
impedes the actions of those who carry out the work.
The cooperative movement is particularly exposed to
departmental adversities and overlapping responsibilities, since its organizational, financial, educational, and specific professional functions are not under
a single department. The only way to avoid the impact of unsteady and often contradictory governmental
impositions is to give certain freedom to regional
and local leaders who are equally familiar with both
the government's objectives and individual local problems. Primary education toward self-administration
on all levels under the guidance of these local leaders is especially important as a balance to bureaucratism and particularism on higher levels.

In India, an organization to promote cooperative

marketing systems without government assistance has been privately initiated. Its expressed purpose is to reduce impeding administrative influences. The view that "a government-oriented cooperative movement would necessarily wipe out the principal aims of cooperation" is expressed in its constitution.

Mr. Eklund, on his visit to the organization's offices during his 1963 inspection tour, received a good impression of the program and activities. He was especially impressed by the formation of an independent credit organization subsidized through American aid.

This example of the emerging forces of self-help in India, where the government's program of centralization fully dominated the beginning of the reestablishment and reorganization of the cooperative movement after the colonial system had been abolished, justifies hope that appropriate education on all levels and prudent encouragement of individuals or groups who are in favor of cooperative emancipation will, as time goes on, counterbalance the initially unavoidable predominance of governmental influence in a growing number of developing countries.

The Food and Agriculture Organization (FAO) of the United Nations, together with representatives of Asian and African countries, has recently organized the Afro-Asian Rural Reconstruction Organization (AARRO), whose main objective is to collect information on the influence of combined political and socioeconomic motives of governments promoting cooperation. The International Federation of Agricultural Producers (IFAP) and the International Cooperative Alliance participate in AARRO's work. The FAO's thoughtful consideration of the problem of government-cooperative relationships is strongly expressed in its report "The Work of FAO to Assist the Development of Cooperatives" (August, 1963), in which the reporter, Ronald H. Gretton, points to the organization's recognition that governmental help is required in the first stages of building cooperative societies, but adds that their social and economic goals are accomplished only when internal forces become dominant.

An even stronger appeal for early education of
members and officers of initially government-
sponsored cooperatives ready for self-administration
has been launched by G. St. Siegens, Director of the
FAO's Cooperatives, Credit, and Rural Sociology
Branch.*

Leaders of several countries where the problem
under review is of immediate significance clearly
recognized the need for finding solutions. A representative of the Ivory Coast Ministry of Agriculture
admitted in his report to the 1962 seminar for African cooperators in Berlin-Tegel, Germany, that the
most acute problem in his country's cooperative development was how to reach the point when, over the
years, the government can slowly withdraw its assistance. In the ensuing discussion, one participant
stated that "cooperatives need state help from the
start to reach maturity, i.e., the spiritual and
material potentialities of self-administration. The
state needs, in the long run, a mature cooperative
movement, i.e., an organization which is able to
promote with its internal forces the cultural and
socioeconomic objectives of a progressive governmental program."

Foreign advisers can do no more than encourage
all tendencies based on this formula. Cautious and
tactful recommendations may be useful where governmental inclinations allow relative freedom for cooperative administrations. But such inclinations can
by no means be taken for granted.

Foreign observers must exert patient and careful consideration of the specifics of individual
government-sponsored cooperative programs before
forming a judgment upon an administration's tendencies. Even the proceedings of highly authoritative

---

*In an article published in the July, 1964, issue
of the FAO's periodical Land Reform under the heading
"Agricultural Cooperatives and State Sponsorship in
Developing Countries," he expands this thesis.

governments in Egypt--for example--may be less contrary to cooperative ideas, if the individual phases
of a comprehensive action are carefully observed,
than might appear to an outsider's over-all impression of the program.

An exceptionally informative illustration of the
individual steps needed and of the versatility required to get a complex program started is given in
the report on the so-called "Nawag" experiment. This
program, launched in Egypt in 1955, is a turning
point in that country's agrarian-reform program. The
report is influenced by the first impression of the
practical lessons learned during the experiment's
progress. Its author, Mahmud Fawzy, the above-
mentioned pioneer of Egyptian agrarian reform, was,
at the time of the Nawag establishment, Director of
the Cooperative Department of the Ministry of Agrarian
Reform in Cairo. The report offers a rare opportunity to both follow the course of an extensive
government-sponsored cooperative program and, specifically, recognize the means resorted to with regard
to the sociological and psychological aspects.

A large-scale investigation of the primary
reasons for an over-all lack of productivity in Egyptian agriculture led the government to decide to organize, as a pioneer project, an agrarian-reform district. In this program, the combined efforts of the
farmers, their existing but inefficient agencies, and
governmental help were to create the conditions required to abolish the structural, technical, financial, and other deficiencies that hampered both agricultural productivity and social progress. Careful
studies to find an appropriate subject for a pioneer
project led to the choice of the village of Nawag as
a representative rural community with most of the
shortcomings characteristic of Egypt's agrarian districts. The Nawag region comprised an average number
of small, uneconomical farm lots, spread over a vast
area, and displaying the typical pattern of Egyptian
agricultural structural defectiveness. Equally
characteristic was the dependence of the Nawag farmers
on moneylenders and local merchants as their exclusive
credit and supply sources. Because the area's

1,200-odd farms were broken up into more than 3,500
single lots, regular irrigation was prevented and
unrelenting erosion continually reduced the already
meager production. An old-type cooperative society
vegetated in the town. Because its membership comprised less than 10 per cent of the neighboring
farmers, it was inefficient and incapable of attracting more members. Nevertheless, the government's
first step was to approach the leaders of the cooperative society in Nawag to give them a general idea
of what the program of structural improvements, regulated irrigation, a system of crop rotation, credit
and supply regulations--all under cooperative control and leadership--would do to put an end to the
existing destructive conditions. Despite the unim-
portance of the society, this approach proved to be
correct, inasmuch as the village sheiks were represented on the supervisory board. Their influence
and authority in rural districts of countries as
Egypt are still powerful and are not hampered by their
involvement in economically unsuccessful undertakings,
such as the Nawag cooperative. The government was
also right in its expectation that the sheiks would
be in favor of the program, not only because they
recognized its soundness but also because they felt
that they could strengthen their role in the community by backing it. Even more important, they could
improve their relationship with the government, which
in Egypt, as in most other rapidly developing Islamic
countries, usually views unfavorably the enduring
pre-eminence of the powerful religious leaders and
institutions, especially where their influence holds
back social progress. Both sides rightly felt that
they had concluded a useful, if not quite spontaneous
pact.

     Next, all the farmers of the district were called
and offered an immediate supply of fertilizers and
seeds, without down payment, at low prices fixed by
the government. Corresponding credits were to be
given at low interest rates--hitherto unknown in the
Nawag region. This offer was based on the condition
that every purchaser join the village cooperative,
submit the use made of the purchased material to the
cooperative's control, and pay for his share as soon

as he sold his crop. Most farmers at the meeting
were eager to take this unique opportunity to get
the badly needed commodities, but entered into stormy
debates on the cooperative's fixed role. The government representative ended the debate by announcing
that fertilizer ordered under the stipulated conditions would be delivered from a nearby warehouse on
the following day to those who stopped arguing.
Prompt fulfillment of this offer resulted in a large
number of farmers joining the cooperative and, in
addition, considerably reduced the formerly dominant
black-market operations in the respective commodities.
The report went on:

> The second step in implementation was to
> spread [the farmers'] confidence, so that
> the initiative might come on their part, to
> demand insecticides for controlling the cot-
> ton worm. . .. When the subject was raised
> at the [second] general meeting, it was ex-
> plained to them that insecticide was poison-
> ous and its use was ineffective in scattered
> holdings besides exposing cattle, poultry,
> and children to accidents, and that in a
> bigger area cultivated by cotton it would be
> more practicable to control pests by the use
> of insecticides.

This information offered the anticipated opportunity to introduce the land-consolidation problem
into the debate. The ensuing discussion of ways to
implement an appropriate program led to presentation
of the first positive proposal, prepared in advance
by agrarian-reform authorities, to combine neighboring blocks into one crop-rotation unit with alter-
nating cotton, rice, and wheat cultivation in three-
year rotation periods. As a first step in ascertaining the feasibility of an experimental rotation principle, a committee of cooperative members and government officials was formed. After several meetings,
it agreed to the selection of some blocks to be combined for cotton and maize cultivation. But when
this decision was presented to a new farmers' meeting
it was rejected because it would interfere with the
rights of ownership.

A period of intensive promotion and instruction
from farm to farm was necessary before another meeting could be held. The 900 farmers in attendance
were at first nearly unanimous in their opposition,
insisting on the individual rights of the owners,
with which the planned regulation would interfere.
Seven hours of discussion were required to break
down their resistance. Finally, a project to regroup
some scattered plots was accepted on condition that
every farmer would be allowed to present his individual objections to the consolidation of specific
blocks, though only if he could present clearly defined reasons. Hiding behind general and abstract
ideas, such as the principle of ownership rights,
was expressly prohibited.

With the help of "exchange committees" in adjust-
ing eventual hardships where the original scheme did
not exactly coincide with specific holdings or where
farmers used to renting some plots feared a loss of
income because of interference by authorities, a plan
was agreed upon and solemnly presented to the Governor of the province by a delegation composed of board
members of the cooperative together with the mayor of
Nawag. This visit had, as the report states it, "a
tremendous effect." The Governor expressed interest
in the "experiment" and promised his help. Although
central-government authorities of a country such as
Egypt need no help from provincial administrations in
continuing a carefully prepared action of far-reaching
significance for the whole country, it was a politically sound idea to get the backing of the provincial
Governor for a radical reform project. To a rural
population, regional administrations often represent
a higher authority than the central government, even
where, as in Egypt, the latter's power is predominant.
People know their Governor and his officials, but
rarely have any contact with representatives of the
highest administration in the distant capital. The
Governor's vote in favor of the Nawag experiment,
which he had not known of before its presentation,
was of great help to local authorities and an encouragement to the farmers involved in the work.
Foreigners may often err in not approaching regional
or local powers when they feel safely authorized by

the highest government authorities. They should always ask in addition for the support of nearby regional or local offices, even when it seems unnecessary. Such contacts avoid the sometimes disturbing resentment of minor officials who, especially in primitive environments, hate to be neglected.

When the practical work in and around Nawag was set into motion, many formerly unforeseen complaints were brought before the exchange committees. Higher or lower productivity of individual lots, their greater or smaller distance from channels or drains, from roads, from the village center, and many similar factors had to be considered. Officials of the Agrarian Reform Cooperative Department had to stay in the district for quite a while to investigate all remaining complaints and to adjust the scheme of consolidation and rotation again and again. A map of the scheme, kept abreast with every detail of the adjustments, was permanently displayed at the door of the mayor's office. This kept everybody informed of what was going on and was an efficient safeguard against suspicions of favoritism and corruption.

During this period, both the village leaders and the cooperative board members were charged by the officials of the Agrarian Reform Cooperative Department with demonstrating their capacity for self-administration by taking over complete control of the remaining work. This proved to be the right approach at the right time. The cooperative leadership improved, and the final stages of the program were implemented without government assistance.

The Nawag experiment not only enriched the technical experience of the agrarian-reform authority, but, even more important, contributed to the practical knowledge of ways and means to overcome the prejudices and misconceptions among the population of a poverty-stricken region, where exploitation and fraud have destroyed confidence and hope, and exaggerated individualism and insistence on more or less fictitious "ownership rights" have perverted the spirit of solidarity and cooperation required to solve common troubles. Now the Nawag experiment is

regarded as a milestone on Egypt's way to progress.
The flexible methods applied succeeded through the
patient adaptation to all technical, sociological,
traditional, and human elements involved. Even the
powerful authority of a strong government and the
best technical and material help must be backed by
individual methods, as applied in Nawag.

The Nawag population--although needy, poorly
educated, economically and socially misled-- was, at
least, familiar with the basically independent status
of a farmer and had some knowledge of cooperative
principles. These factors had to be considered by
the program leaders and even contributed to their
difficulties. Much greater difficulties, however,
must be faced when hitherto totally suppressed peoples
are involved in agrarian reform. After his extended
visit to the Egyptian cooperative establishments in
1962, the Minister of Agriculture of the German state
of Hessen, Dr. Tassilo Troescher, described the
graveness of this sociological problem in his report
to the Friedrich Ebert Foundation, Bonn, the sponsor
of his and this author's common research study.

> Egypt's fellahs [peasant workers] are cul-
> tivating the land in the same way as 5,000
> years ago. . . . Their poverty and exploi-
> tation has not changed over the millennia.
> These men are now engaged by the government
> to cooperate in the framework of the Agra-
> rian Reform Law. The constant concern ex-
> pressed by the Egyptian leaders is how to
> gain the confidence of these people, whose
> mistrust of all representatives of authority
> stems from the eternal suppression to which
> they have been subjected, regardless of the
> existing political and social structure.
> Freeing the fellahs from their subjugation
> under reckless landlords and elevating them
> to the status of landowners may endanger
> the country's internal stability. The sud-
> den effortless liberation of masses of
> people ignorant of how to act in freedom is
> regarded by leaders of the reform work with
> considerable anxiety.

The liberation of men from slavelike conditions is certainly one of the most urgent duties of our time. But the seriousness of the inherent problems is often not fully recognized. Enthusiastic promoters of modernization frequently fail to perceive the underlying psychological and political difficulties that, to a large extent, account for the strong and often rather dictatorial methods applied by some governments, especially in Africa, for keeping under control the political and social transformations they set in motion. Most of the reports, protocols, and memoranda in the research material used in this book reflect the problem, especially for cooperative leaders, of how to overcome the prevailing human weakness of a people to be educated for a new life, whose values they are at first unable to appreciate. Some examples of native leaders' concern over their people's condition may be cited.

A Nigerian leader points to the problem of converting his people's predominant fatalism and mistrust into confidence and hope for a better future through cooperation and mutual help. Initiative and social awareness are, in the eyes of an Ivory Coast representative, the elements of progress expected to be developed by means of cooperation and before the consequences of "colonial enslavement" can cease. A Greek cooperator sees the peasants' resistance to technical progress, which he blames on their fear of anything that might raise the unemployment level, as one of the most serious obstacles to cooperative success. A leading farmer from Pakistan reports on the peasants' sluggish working habits and the difficulty of arousing any desire to control their own destiny.

More general appeals for honesty, for defeating corruption, for reducing all kinds of fraud are expressed in many other reports. All these remarks point to the human obstacles to be overcome and to the fact that most native leaders are well aware of the internal psychological and sociological aspects of development problems.

Foreign advisers will succeed in winning the confidence of native leaders only if they accommodate

their technical programs to the human and other specific conditions that characterize the people and
the region. The patience required to postpone seemingly urgent technical improvements in favor of educational and similar preparation and to make the individuals involved fit for the work is rewarded by
trustful cooperation.

How deeply representatives of developing countries appreciate foreigners' showing consideration
for their individual problems was demonstrated at a
lecture on cooperative finance during the 1962 seminar for African cooperators in Berlin. Professor
A. Hirschfeld, of the Institute of Cooperative Research in Paris, addressed a group of native leaders
who listened attentively but without expression to
his discussion of the administrative and organizational functions of banking, the specifics of agricultural credit, and related matters. Toward the
end of the lecture, Professor Hirschfeld remarked
that, notwithstanding the care required for appropriate technical means, "more human than financial
problems are involved" in the credit business, especially if it is to be organized cooperatively. At
this sentence, a storm of applause broke out, expres-
sing the audience's satisfaction with the emphasis on
the nontechnical aspects.

The ILO stresses the striking difference between
the methods required to build cooperative establishments for new settlers and hitherto-landless wage
earners and those for groups of independent but primitive farmers or craftsmen.

The variety of motivations, goals, and--to no
lesser degree--obstacles that governments of developing countries visualize or encounter in the non-
agrarian areas of their economies are often induced
by political aspirations and reflect objectives or
result in formations without parallels in Western
cooperative movements. The cooperative form is often
chosen, for instance, to solve the difficulties
caused by the sudden abandonment of foreign enterprises after the establishment of political autonomy,
or by the new government's issuance of laws that

prohibit or gravely hamper foreign businesses. The
immediate goal of reorganizing the abandoned firms
or agencies is to avoid complete stoppages in economically important fields of production, trade, and
related services, and to prevent unemployment among
native workers and employees of the respective enterprises. These enterprises are mostly small and
medium-sized firms formerly owned or managed by for-
eigners--too small to be taken over by a governmental
agency or otherwise not suitable for immediate appro-
priation.

The announcement of such a reorganization is a
politically opportune instrument of propaganda. It
gives the impression of fulfilling the promise of
liberation from foreign exploitation but at the same
time avoids arousing the suspicion that confiscation
of foreign enterprises is a first step toward total
nationalization. Continuing the foreigners' businesses as a cooperative may also be seen as demonstrating
the government's confidence in the people's capacity
for active participation in their country's progressive plans. Finally, the government's need to demonstrate to Western countries its intention of developing self-administrative capacities may contribute to
the choice of a cooperative for administering confis-
cated foreign firms. Such a demonstration may particularly be sought by predominantly socialistic
governments that want to retain Western aid by prov-
ing they are non-Communist.

Often, however, neither the substance of the
enterprise nor the relationship between the involved
people--workers, employees, clients, suppliers--meet
the requirements of cooperative tasks. In a milk-
pasteurization plant in Cairo, for instance, as well
as in a glass factory in Alexandria, none of the
native personnel was able to organize the work, to
operate the machines, or to prevent the immediate
shortage of raw materials and spare parts. A longer
stoppage was required until these problems were
solved. Meanwhile, the staff received modest salary
rates with a much better future promised to those who
would stay on and adjust to the new order replacing
the former "principle of exploitation" and inspiring

everyone by the prevailing spirit of "common interest
of all." A basic introduction to cooperative ideas
and rules was combined with a notice that small salary deductions were necessary in order to build up
the member-employees' contribution to the share capital of the cooperative society. The author had no
opportunity to ascertain the workers' reaction, but
an official's report stated that a "unanimous accord
from all sides" had been reached. Some larger suppliers and clients of the firms agreed to join relatively easily, when they understood that continued
business was dependent upon their joining. By these
means, and with the help of loans from public funds,
operations started once again, closely supervised by
government-appointed managers and local authorities.

A representative of the Central Organization of
Industrial Cooperatives admitted that, after the
first few years of operation, whether the cooperative
form would be preserved was still an open question.
Continued production and employment of workers and
employees had been achieved, but a truly cooperative
spirit was lacking, despite efforts made by regular
membership meetings, lectures, and other educational
programs. This new type of "cooperative" would remain, in the representative's opinion, a burden to
the Central Organization for many years to come.

An example observed in Alexandria illustrates
an unforeseen development. This was the establishment of an organization more like a trade union than
a genuine cooperative. Various groups of workmen in
the harbor, mainly weighers and loaders, were employed by private, mostly foreign, agencies, which
served sellers and buyers of cotton by ascertaining
the weight and quality of the cotton packs arriving
from the interior for export. The certificates issued by the agents were binding for both sellers and
buyers, and so business was based on the personal
confidence inspired by individual agents. In order
to preserve the harbor of Alexandria as one of the
most important cotton trade centers in the world,
foreign agencies of the kind described above were
allowed to remain in business. However, steps were
initiated to organize experienced workmen and

employees, who were temporarily unemployed, in a cooperative society whose object was to take over the business of the private agencies. But cotton sellers and buyers preferred to continue the tested relationship with the agencies who had their confidence, and the weighers and loaders' cooperative society was left with the relatively small government transactions performed in the port. There was not even enough work for the temporarily unemployed men, and the propaganda originally planned to induce the employees of the private agencies to join the cooperative was useless. In addition, the private agents reacted to the propaganda with small wage increases, with the result that very few workers joined the cooperative.

The cooperative decided that some kind of agreement must be reached with the private agents in order to secure at least some justification for the new organization. It finally was recognized as the official representative of all harbor workers, but prohibited from competing for any business other than government transactions and from interfering with the agents' employment practices, except where intervention was required. Although the cooperative failed to reach an agreement on compulsory membership, voluntary membership was more than 50 per cent after the first year of the settlement. Only a minority, however, were active in the cooperative's shipping operations; the majority, whether employed by one of the agencies or temporarily unemployed, regarded the society as merely the protector of their interests. In this sense, the cooperative resembled labor unions in Western countries. This originally unforeseen development was tolerated by the central authorities as a step toward better working conditions in general, and also as a potential opportunity to bring social education to hitherto-uneducated people.

In the early 1960's, the Egyptian Government discussed plans to organize groups of road and construction workers cooperatively in order to release them from their often ruinous dependence upon ruthless private contractors. This plan had to be postponed because the financial burden of supplying

transportation and lodging for the workers proved to
be too heavy. Without these, they would remain subject to the contractors' mercy. This reason appeared
to the author as more a pretext than a decisive hin-
drance when juxtaposed against the hesitation, expressed by competent officials, to establish a
hitherto-unknown type of collective work society.
This would be accomplished by installing road workers
in independent groups, away from controlling centers,
and initiate politically undesirable imitations among
the urban population. The idea under consideration
was to acquire some experience in cooperative labor
societies by studying already existing institutions
of a similar type in a neighboring country. Some reliable workers were to be chosen for these studies
for the later formation of an elite group for the establishment of road and other construction-work cooperatives.

The motivations for establishing worker cooperatives in Greece should be mentioned again. The basic
reason, of course, is the disastrously high rate of
unemployment in almost all rural districts of Greece.
As a consequence, younger peasants tend to look for
work in the cities, where they swell the ranks of unemployed urban masses. The program of creating rural
jobs to avoid an influx into the cities should also
strengthen the agricultural marketing and supply cooperatives by establishing processing plants manned
by jobless rural workers. Workshops and facilities
for their instruction and education must be set up
before modern cleaning, sorting, packing, and similar
machines can be used. The Greek farmers and their
cooperatives are, in general, not in favor of modernization and are certainly unable to finance long-term
and expensive projects. The twofold benefits of the
program, however--the settlement of jobless peasants
in rural areas and the improvement and enlargement
of the cooperatives' production--are too evident to
omit any effort to get it under way.

The need to settle vagrant workers was also the
basic reason for organizing cooperative farms in
Guinea. Annually, masses of workers used to go across
the border to neighboring Senegal for seasonal work.

To keep them busy at home, settlement cooperatives were established, in which new kinds of agricultural products were cultivated. In this way, close to 10,000 former migrant workers were permanently settled shortly after 1959.

A different settlement problem led to an industrial cooperative experiment in Egypt. The problem was how a rural industrial plant could successfully compete in order to keep its skilled labor against the lure of the city.

The Misr Spinning and Weaving Company in El Mahalla el Kobra, Egypt, one of the country's largest enterprises, originally British-owned, tried to solve its settlement problem by announcing, in 1960, that it would "cooperate with its workers and employees in establishing a cooperative society for domestic industries that it supplied with all means of success such as funds, machinery, and technical experts. The aim is to give employment to the workers' sons and families, increase their income, and occupy their time for their benefit."[2]

There was, however, much more involved (and soon accomplished) than was expressed in this modest sentence. Two main functions were cooperatively organized and performed separately (although under one administrative roof): 1) rug knitting and weaving in a common workshop by children ranging from ten to fourteen years of age, and 2) all kinds of needlework performed in their homes by the female members of the workmen's families. The children were allowed to join the workshop only if they attended the public school regularly. This was socially important, since in Egypt, children were kept home under all kinds of pretexts despite the legal obligation to attend school. Because both parents and children around the Misr Company's plants were eager to become members of the cooperative society, the children went to school regularly.

The primary reason for the rapidly growing interest in the new experiment lies in the effect of the new methods used to teach the children rug knitting

and combined methods of group work. Also, they received a vivid introduction to mutual help and collaboration, plus the incentive of a small merit
bonus. The children were registered as regular members after an apprenticeship of one to two years,
during thich they had to prove their mastery in all
areas of the work, including designs patterned after
ancient rug pieces. They then could choose between
continuing to work in the cooperative workshop or
switching to their home. In the latter case, necessary tools were supplied to them on credit. Marketing
of the products, whether made in the workshop or at
home, was left exclusively to the society, making
the members independent of ruthless private merchants.
In two years, the cooperative established good contacts with reliable dealers and also with foreign
importers of Oriental articles. The incoming money
was divided, after current expenses were paid, between amortization of the initial loans granted for
a workshop and the equipment, and distribution to
the members.

     Similar methods were applied to the women work-
ing at home. They were admitted to membership on
probation and, if necessary, received an initial term
of instruction. They were also taught old techniques
of needlework and long-forgotten ancient patterns,
which were brought to the cooperative's director by
appointed experts or came from a museum. The women
take pride in this quality work. When a piece is
finished, it is presented to the supervisor and, if
judged satisfactory, put on sale in one of the cooperative's exhibition rooms. An advance payment is
given to the women immediately, later to be accounted
for with final distribution of the realized profit.
The advance is usually higher than the total price
formerly paid by private merchants.

     The effect of all these arrangements and the
treatment of women as community members with equal
rights greatly enhanced their status in the family
and in the neighborhood. In this way, the women and
children were induced not to look to large cities
for better living conditions, educational opportunities, and more entertainment. The men, in addition

to welcoming the higher family income, were gratified
to observe the contentment of the members of their
family, and learned the benefits accruing from cooperative work.

All these factors worked together to bind the
workers closer to the factory in El Mahallah--the
original goal of its management in starting the costly experiment. However, the success of the experiment was due to a rare combination of propitious circumstances, mainly the great vision of the factory's
general manager, his knowledge of and keen interest
in the country's traditional techniques, his social
awareness, and his devotion to the new government's
program of socioeconomic progress, and finally the
financial strength of his corporation, which made it
possible to risk considerable amounts of money in a
risky undertaking. This, however, does not detract
from the achievements of the establishment, which
show, in addition to the genuine goal of settling the
factory's labor resources, how primitive people can
be led to work toward new goals and objectives if the
material and ideal means are rightly coordinated and
adapted to the human and vocational conditions of the
individuals involved.

The by-product of the El Mahallah experiment--
the early practical education of children in cooperative activities and conceptions--is of particular
importance. The many instances where school cooperatives are established demonstrate an increasing recognition by cooperative leaders that an early start
of such an education is necessary in view of the
often prevailing prejudices among the older people,
their traditionalism, their mistrust of everything
new, their lack of imagination. The children's experience in school cooperatives are often convincing
to their parents.

Various types of school cooperatives were established relatively early in Greece, Cyprus, Egypt,
and more recently in several Latin American countries.
Cyprus is an outstanding example of organized education for thrift. The school cooperatives' savings
compete with the deposits of regular cooperatives,

and are deposited, together with the latter, in a
central bank. This joint deposit represents a large
contribution to the total funds available for the
country's cooperative movement.

The goals of the several hundred Greek school
cooperatives are more immediately directed toward
the individual interests of various groups of children. They mostly perform garden and handicraft
work. The products are sold cooperatively, and the
income is used for books and teaching materials, for
occasional excursions and celebrations, and often
for the support of needy classmates. The pupils are
taught to perform all administrative functions of
their society by themselves, and the teachers act as
"consultants" only, without a voice. Preparation for
later membership in agricultural and industrial cooperatives is a declared objective.

The school cooperatives in the two large cities
of Egypt, Cairo and Alexandria, were in a state of
transition at the time of the author's visit. They
were privately established before the government
started its efforts to promote general cooperation.
Their more systematic development was planned in connection with a program to make "cooperation" a regular subject in all elementary schools as soon as
enough teachers were properly trained. No information was available on the work performed by the more
than fifty registered school cooperatives in the two
Egyptian cities, where they were officially placed
under the supervision of the industrial cooperative
authority.

The Organization of the American States (OAS)
has reported on the considerable progress achieved
in the school cooperative movement of various South
American countries. In 1961, the Brazilian State of
Pernambuco had 56,000 pupils organized in 126 cooperatives; other states followed the Pernambuco
lead. The director of the OAS' Cooperative Department, Fernando Chaves, emphasized that the idealistic
goals of the movement were designed "to plant in the
children's minds the ideals of solidarity and mutual
help," but has privately agreed with the author that

much more should and could be achieved if more attention was given to teacher preparation, including the
basic elements of cooperative education. Foreign
advisers should stress this point whenever programs
of cooperative education are discussed. Sometimes
such proposals are not well received by cooperative
leaders in developing countries. They tend to regard
the advisers' role as strictly technical and feel
that suggestions on education exceed their assignment
and intrude on the internal affairs of a foreign
country.

Such resistance is illustrated specifically in
the often inevitable discussion of the best way to
educate the women to become active contributors to
the cooperative program. Despite the inferior status
of women in many developing countries, their influence
in the family, mainly on the children, is usually
strong enough to offset the strides taken toward cooperative development by the men. Also of great importance is the use of women by reactionary religious
leaders to undermine the effectiveness of cooperative
organizations.

The exact opposite situation can be found where
the first signs of female emancipation become evident.
It is obvious that the cooperative movement offers
many opportunities to help women achieve equal rights.
This is well understood by more advanced women in
developing countries. As a result, they are usually
active in organizing cooperatives of female workers.
In some larger cities of the Middle East, where foreign tourists looking for genuine native products
are often victimized by dishonest "bazaar" traders,
cooperative societies can protect both the tourists
from fraud and the native artisans from exploitation.

The leaders of these organizations are both experienced in craft trades and educated in social
work. They go to see the women in their homes, teach
them how to produce salable wares, inspect the sur-
roundings, and try to improve their over-all living
conditions. In Cairo, one of these cooperatives runs
an exhibition and sales store stocked with high-
quality goods. It also provides day care for the

children of members who otherwise would have neither the space nor the time to work properly.

Cooperative organizations help women achieve emancipation in various ways. In Guinea, for instance, 1,500 women work in a dyers' cooperative society. In Nigeria, where the wives of small farmers originally worked only as bearers of vegetables and fruits to the market, a regular marketing cooperative has been established. The members exchange and sort the produce, agreeing upon assortments, weights, and prices. The women thus become partners in their husbands' business.

The relatively modest ascendancy of women's cooperatives, combined with the secondary impact of their husbands', children's, and neighbors' cooperative work, contributes inevitably to a general desire to improve the status of women in developing countries. Of great influence in this drive are diplomatic wives living in the West or attending various international meetings and conferences. Also of great importance are the wives and daughters of upper-echelon families. In many cases, these women have been educated in Europe or America, and are deeply aware of the vast difference existing between East and West in regard to the status of women.

One woman in a Middle Eastern country, in charge of organizing women's cooperatives, spoke to the author of the "forgotten woman" in all efforts to improve social conditions in developing nations. She characterized the still prevailing "exploitation" of women as a no lesser evil than past "exploitation" by foreigners and usurers, and condemned her own government's habit of blaming outside forces for all problems, thereby disregarding the inherent weakness in suppressing the female population. She expressed a firm desire to use her influence as a cooperative leader to awaken all women to recognition of their low status and to lead them to achieve equal rights.

The remarks of a practicing woman physician in Cairo--a member of Parliament--were equally significant, though less radical. She also pointed to the efforts to improve the education of only the men, disregarding the paramount need to lift the slavelike status of women, especially in the rural districts and in most peasant families.

The wife of an Indian delegate, who participated with her husband in a seminar of the German Foundation for Developing Countries, pointed to the urgency of breaking down the widespread resistance to enlightening Indian women on birth control, and said she would use women's cooperative societies, of which she was a leader, to educate the members in the use of contraceptives.

An Iranian woman, a member of her country's delegation to the seminar, added that cooperative organizations should extend their educational efforts toward making as many women as possible, directly or indirectly connected with the cooperative movement, free from religious influences that not only block their knowledge of birth control but are also one of the major obstacles to female education in the Arab world.

These observations give the impression that cooperative establishments will be welcomed and used by advanced groups of women in developing countries as vehicles for promoting equal rights of women regardless of the opinion of native leaders, foreign advisers, or any other authority. This originally unforeseen consequence of creating cooperative organizations will certainly add to the internal difficulties in many regions. In view of the political and social emotions aroused in the Western world during the long struggle for emancipation, the reactions of societies with the majority of women still far behind the nineteenth-century pre-emancipation status of the American and European female must surely be vehement.

In order to mitigate the passions accompanying the controversy over women's rights, especially in cooperatives, it seems advisable to dispense in principle with the idea that any prior resistance could be useful. The movement can be brought under control only by establishing friendly relations and close bonds between the leading authorities of cooperative organizations and the promoters of women's progress. Regional groups of experts, including well-educated women, may best prepare "cooperation" through a quiet adaptation of necessary reforms in this delicate field of evolution, thus preventing its degeneration into a minor revolution.

In general, cooperative establishments in the non-agrarian sector of a developing country's economy are neither so well established nor so efficient as those with an agricultural orientation.

When the Egyptian Government established a central organization for industrial cooperatives--as had previously been done for agricultural and consumer cooperatives--the motivations and plans were different. The program for the agricultural organization was dictated by the predominance of the agrarian-reform program, and the plan to administer the consumer cooperatives was based on the need to keep in business stores in Cairo and Alexandria formerly owned by foreigners. The government felt that these enterprises must continue to supply the public with textiles and household goods that they could not buy elsewhere. Concern about the potential unemployment of the stores' employees was also a major consideration.

In contrast, no such predetermined course of action existed for industry. Between 130 and 140 cooperative units had been organized privately prior to 1960, mainly by craftsmen who cooperatively exhibited and sold their products--metal, wood, leather, and ivory work in the traditional Oriental style, rugs and other weaving and knitting products. These cooperatives had to register as members of the Central Organization of Industrial Cooperatives, which, until several years after their registration, had no program other than a vague idea of working toward "coordination, extension, financial reorganization, and education." The Central Organization's primary goal was to build a new type of cooperative by using the skilled labor of all industry to advance government plans for industrialization. For this purpose,

some "training centers" were established; the ultimate goal was 200 such centers, in as many areas as
possible.

The link between this program of technical education of young workers and the establishment of cooperative units was, according to the explanation of
an organization leader, the prospective transformation of the centers into cooperative societies when
they would seem "to be ripe for self-administration."
Until then, the centers were merely technical schools
under governmental leadership. The author raised
the question of membership and cooperative education
in preparation for the future transformation, since
it is difficult to imagine how a number of workers,
trained in a school and leaving for jobs in distant
areas after finishing their technical training, could
fulfill the conditions of cooperative membership.
The answers to this and related questions were disappointing and showed a certain preoccupation by government officials with the potential inconvenience of
giving too much independence to factory workers who
would primarily live in or near cities and who could
possibly form the nuclei of undesirable elements
among the urban population. Similar preoccupations
are found among the leaders of most countries with
centralized government and large masses of poor workers living in urban centers. This uneasiness, however,
does not solve the problem of building cooperatives,
where, as in Egypt, the decision has been made to
organize the skilled workers cooperatively.

Under the influence of the general program of
"cooperation," as expressed in Egyptian constitutional
law, a combination of incompatible factors was in
evidence. The author did not conceal his belief that
the program of transforming the training centers into
cooperatives should be abandoned for the time being,
to be revived only when skilled workers formed their
own cooperative societies (group work, supply, marketing, or whatever other joint function) and were
prepared to run the training centers in order to extend their self-administered activities into actual
professional education.

The same concern over a premature development
of urban cooperatives into independent units was apparently at the bottom of the program to bring the
already existing craftsmen, merchants, and small
shopowners cooperatives under permanent control. An
example of this concern was displayed by the following
scheme presented to the author when he interviewed
the head of the industrial organization: a number of
district cooperatives were to be established, completely financed by the state, and contributing to
the individual cooperatives' income under the condition that the latter admit the district cooperatives
as shareholders and concede the right of employing
their managers. This regulation was not expressed in
the statutes or bylaws of the individual cooperatives,
but was to be settled individually as part of the
credit arrangements. In order to avoid any conflict
with the cooperative law, which, of course, does not
allow cooperative societies to be deprived of their
right to employ managers, this type of settlement
was chosen. The program will, in all probability,
prevent any marked further extension of the industrial
cooperative movement in Egypt if the central organization does not recognize its impracticability.

A cooperative system in the industrial sector,
based on the above plan, would be contrary to the
system applied in the agrarian sector of Egypt's
economy, where the local units are expected to accumulate the capital required to become shareholders
of the planned district societies, thus conforming
to the principle of building the cooperative pyramid
from local units upward to the top of the organization. The author's reference to these facts seemingly did not impress the officials, who, however, did
not oppose his reasoning either. They gave an impression of unconcern regarding an eventual restraint
of industrial cooperative developments in Egypt.

A positive although indirect course of promotion
is followed by the Cameroun Government, as described
in a report presented to the International Cooperative
Training Center in Madison, Wisconsin, at its 1963
spring seminar. Cameroun's industrial cooperatives

are of different types: supply and marketing societies of tailors, butchers, cabinetmakers, and fishermen. They were individually and privately organized and did not grow into a coordinated movement.
The government first took an active interest when it
became necessary to combine in cooperative form the
existing coffee-roasting and -sorting plants, which
individually were too small to use the modern machines
necessary for obtaining the quality of coffee required for export. Since coffee is the principal export commodity in Cameroun, the government made every
effort to establish some coffee-processing cooperatives, despite considerable opposition from private
owners of small hand-operated roasting plants. Because of this resistance, the government decided
against any further initiative to organize individual
branches cooperatively and, instead, to concentrate
on promoting cooperative credit societies for small
handicraft and trade units. The State Bank of
Cameroun provides the credit funds, and membership in
the credit cooperatives is expected to be attractive
enough to overcome the general prejudice against organizations that remind the people of the colonial
Sociétés de Prévoyance. The government hopes that
other types of cooperative societies can be organized
after the benefits of access to cheap money, not attainable outside the cooperative society, become evident. The government also hopes that the continuing
success of the coffee-processing cooperatives will
demonstrate how conditions can be improved by combining small plants into workable units.

    A more favorable attitude toward industrial co-
operative organization has been observed among different groups in Nigeria. Dr. Waidelich, director
of the cooperative school in Stuttgart-Hohenheim,
studied the Nigerian cooperative movement in 1962,
and he reports on the success of various professional
groups in organizing cooperative societies. He cites
the cooperative established by woodcutting craftsmen
to train young people in the country's traditional
woodwork. A similar objective led a number of weavers, mostly women, to work together cooperatively.
This society also demonstrates that cooperatives,
even small ones, can meet both professional and social

needs. One area of the plant is reserved for expec-
tant and young mothers. This step, just as much as
the material results of production and sale, greatly
contributes to the success of the enterprises.

The Greek Government's program to settle jobless
peasants in rural districts by attaching processing
plants to the marketing cooperatives in various parts
of the country was usually not well received by the
farmers themselves. The farmers were generally dis-
trustful of innovations. However, their reluctance
to contract additional debts for the new installations did not completely block the program. Regret-
tably, at least 51 per cent of the cooperatives'
share capital remains permanently reserved for state
participation, in recognition that the government put
up the initial capital for installing the processing
plants. Thus, some oil-extracting plants, wine-
pressing installations, refineries, mills, and resin
factories have been established, and fertilizer factories and cold storage houses have been planned.
These are all set up as cooperatives, although initiated and administered by state authorities. An
educational leader of the Greek cooperative movement
expressed hope that the formation of training centers
near the new processing plants, where the young peasants undergo technical and mental education, may convince the government relatively soon that majority
control can be transferred to the active members.

A contrasting picture of the success of private
initiative in establishing new forms of industrial
cooperatives in some South American countries is given
in the 1964 AID report to the U.S. Congress. The
initiative of persons with detailed knowledge of specific community needs produced an alliance of small
private and larger industrial interests that led to
new means of cooperation. When the road-construction
program of the Bolivian Government connected a very
poor region with a more developed section, a transport
society was established. However, it failed to raise
enough money to provide trucks and other vehicles.
One of the leaders approached a car-manufacturing
plant in a distant part of the country and obtained
its agreement to join the society. The factory

supplied two trucks as the initial share capital of the cooperative. As an immediate consequence, the cooperative gained more members. Their payments, modest at first, soon enabled the organization to start regular transportation on a limited schedule, which had to be extended. This successful arrangement led the factory to make similar contracts with cooperatives in other communities. It found, in this way, a new field for expanded production.

More examples were reported by AID. A motor manufacturer contracted with a fishing cooperative to supply small motor engines enabling the fishermen to expand their field of operations. Leaders in Nicaragua, Colombia, and Ecuador discovered stocks of obsolete instruments, tools, and small machines in industrial enterprises; although these items had been superseded by more modern ones, they were still usable for various purposes in the cooperatives' workshops. Some electricity cooperatives were able to buy obsolete transformers at extremely low prices. Dairy cooperatives increased their efficiency and attracted new members after they acquired inexpensive centrifuges.

A primary goal of American missions in developing countries is to help individual cooperators acquire the initiative and inventiveness required to perform such progressive work. The impact of this approach on the spirit of cooperative leaders and on the movement's growth in the industrial sector of the Latin American economy is not to be underrated, even though individual cases may appear to be insignificant in themselves.

It is difficult to discuss the motivations and goals underlying the establishment and promotion of consumer cooperatives in developing countries in the same sense as the formation of agricultural and industrial cooperatives was considered earlier in this chapter. Neither immediate population requirements nor specific government programs brought consumer cooperatives into existence. There were specific circumstances and reasons different from those that inspire regular cooperative programs, organizing

cooperatives in countries, for instance, like Cyprus,
Cameroun, Egypt, and some Latin American areas. These
are not only the author's observations. Experienced
American experts fully agree. These observations
justify the prediction that "consumer cooperatives
would"--contrary to the history of the cooperative
movement in the Western world--"not be the first, but
the last, form of cooperation to be introduced to
developing countries."[3]

In Cameroun, where no cooperatives at all existed, the first consumer cooperative was established in
1945, immediately after World War II, when an acute
shortage of food and most consumer goods plagued the
country. Because there was no adequate private or
government organization to distribute food and other
supplies, a cooperative-like self-help organization
was improvised.

In Burma and Ceylon, the governments have encouraged the formation of consumer cooperative shops
as a weapon against then-existing monopolies of foreign import firms. Government-owned wholesale societies were established, and they accumulated large
quantities of consumer goods, whose distribution was
expected to be best performed by a widespread chain of
shops administered by individuals. Israeli advisers are
said to have proposed similar organizations in various
African countries, but they had no success in establishing regular cooperative retail activities.

In 1957 and 1958, the sequestration of British
and French tea import firms in Egypt, which until
then had monopolized this business, provided an opportunity to expand the retail operations of these
chain stores by permitting them to distribute all
kinds of food supplies. The stores were thus able to
supply consumer-cooperative services to the urban
population. After it was reorganized as a cooperative
organization, the tea business, always a source of
high profits in Egypt, made possible a general price
reduction and the creation of a competitive market.
Private traders were forced to reduce their prices.
As a result, cooperative membership increased; nonetheless, more than half of the customers in Cairo and

Alexandria were (until 1962 at least) nonmembers.

Visits to larger installations of the consumer cooperatives in Cairo, plus a talk with the leader of the government Central Organization, confirmed the author's impression that although the initial goal of preventing an interruption in the stores' supply functions and enlarging their programs to create a competitive market was successful, the success was based exclusively on government planning. A project to extend the operation into rural districts, where consumer shops would be attached to already existing agricultural marketing and supply cooperatives, met with failure due to departmental liabilities and credit problems. More serious evidence of the customers' prevailing indifference, among both members and nonmembers, was the random assortment of household goods in the shops and at the cooperatives' exhibition in Heliopolis, near Cairo; the displays of furniture, textiles, and apparel showed neither the solid form and quality of Oriental tradition nor the taste and functional requirement of modern production. They resembled poor imitations of foreign models; moreover, they were too bulky to be used in the modern housing developments in Egypt, which, as elsewhere, offer limited space. The leader of the Central Organization accepted these criticisms, but pointed to his agency's inability to overcome the dominating influence of some importers and manufacturers over the organization's purchasing agents. Quality controls apply only to foodstuff and medicines, but it is planned to extend them to all goods handled by the shops. At the time of the author's investigation, the question of forming committees of members to voice their needs and appraise the quality of stocked goods or that offered by suppliers had not been considered. The leader's reaction to this suggestion plainly reflected his view that the members showed neither the necessary interest nor the capacity to perform this truly cooperative function.

The numerous consumer cooperative societies in Latin American countries can usually be traced back to the initiative of welfare organizations or workers'

unions, according to the chief of the Cooperative
Department of the OAS, Mr. Chaves. In Argentina,
Chile, and Uruguay, where certain mutual-help societies have been established, steps were taken to
transform them into cooperative units under the leadership of the original founders. Similarly, the initiative of union leaders in Mexico and Brazil led to
the establishment of consumer cooperatives; in 1964,
the former had more than 1,400, the latter about
1,300. The movement has quickly grown into one of
continental scope.

An initial conference of consumer cooperative
leaders from all countries of the American continent
met in Puerto Rico in 1963. This conference reflected an urgent need to end the usurpation of private
monopolies, which still prevail in most Latin American countries. In many of these regions, efforts are
being made to solve educational problems, primarily
for local leadership, with the help of special institutions attached to state universities. The students
are trained in the detail work of membership recruitment and education in all areas of the countries involved.

A basic reason for the failure of consumer cooperatives to be as popular in developing countries as
other cooperatives is their nonprofessional character.
Peasants, craftsmen, traders, and small shopkeepers
are quite easily convinced of the usefulness of joint
action to improve production, to obtain the advantages
of joint buying and selling, and to employ cooperative
services that are not attainable individually. In
contrast to professional objectives, the consumer
cooperative is based on the readiness to work together
in the private sector of life and, to a certain degree, invades the individual household of its members
by providing them with daily supplies. This concept
is basically opposed to the individualistic tendencies of most people in the developing countries, and
so an enthusiastic reception cannot be expected.

The motivations and goals underlying cooperative
housing programs are too diversified in the areas
under discussion to allow the author to draw significant conclusions related to the specific theme of this

book. Some personal observations, together with reports from people involved in cooperative housing programs in different countries, lead to a tentative general conclusion that two factors are paramount in cooperative housing projects:

First, housing facilities must be appropriate for the prospective tenants. Units built with only ultimate cooperative objectives in mind (settlement in newly developed rural districts, village population enlargement, slum eradication in cities) are not necessarily appropriate. For example, modern homes with the newest design are totally unsuitable for people who have just been living in urban slums, primitive rural areas, or as nomads. They are unacquainted with, and intimidated by, modern appliances, and may be troubled by the immediate proximity of others. Education and a slow process of assimilation are necessary to acclimate the new tenants to their new conditions and the relative luxury of their new homes. Such psychological and sociological problems are seen in cooperative housing projects to a degree, possibly higher, than in other forms of cooperative organization.

Second, the general observation that cooperative housing developments frequently do not attain their goals either technically or financially reflects many planners' failures to combine technical knowledge with social insight. This failure is primarily evident when private contractors are hired to build cooperative housing units and are not supervised sufficiently.

An interesting report by Professor Hassan Fathy, a prominent Egyptian architect who has been active in rural cooperative building programs, cites the pitfalls in hiring private contractors for cooperative building projects.[4] The report points to their ignorance of cooperative goals as a source of continuing trouble and as the main cause of many failures. Professor Fathy recommends that the future residents actively participate in the construction work, and that admission to membership be based on the amount of work performed instead of monetary

contributions to the share capital. These requirements would give the members practical awareness of
what cooperative self-help can do and prepare them
for community living.

NOTES TO CHAPTER 2

1. Mahmud Fawzy, address to a technical conference on "Cooperatives in the Near East" (English
version) (Cairo, Egypt: Al-Kahira Printing House),
p. 5.

2. Misr Spinning and Weaving Company, Annual
Report, 1960 (Cairo, Egypt: Imprimerie Misr, 1961).

3. International Labor Office, "The Role of
Cooperatives in the Economic and Social Development
of Developing Countries" (in English and German; part
of the Preparatory Report for the 1964 and 1966 conferences) (Geneva, Switzerland: ILO, 1964), p. 35.

4. "Rural Self-Help Housing," International
Labour Review, Geneva, 1962.

CHAPTER **3** THE CASE FOR AND
AGAINST COOPERATIVE-
COLLECTIVE PRODUCTION

Next to the problem of how to avoid lasting
government influence and control, considered in the
preceding chapter, ranks the problem of whether cooperatives for collective production should be established in developing countries. Both problems
raise the identical concern of endangering the final
goals of cooperation. The Western idea of cooperation is to benefit small units of production by taking over such auxiliary operations as buying, selling, and financing, thereby strengthening the independence of individual producers by freeing them
to deal only with actual production. This concept
seems irreconcilable with collectivism, which destroys individual ownership and responsibility.

It is generally recognized that, at least for
the present, only state leadership can give momentum
to cooperative movements in developing countries.
But no such unanimity exists regarding collective
production. Opinions are divided on the need to establish collectively producing cooperatives in order
to improve farming techniques. How to avoid the destructive consequences of collectivism once it is
introduced in any sector of production is a subject
of heated debate.

In its Preparatory Report for the 1965 and 1966
Plenary Sessions on Cooperative Establishment in
Developing Countries, the ILO listed without comment
workmen's, craftsmen's, and farmers' productive cooperative societies among the potential forms of applying cooperative methods. This is not meant to mini-
mize the dangers involved in collective production,

nor does it express the ILO's acceptance of the
trend toward collectivism in certain member states.
Rather, it reflects the ILO's position that theories
and abstract principles cannot lead to sound judgments either way, and that sociological conditions
of a particular region at a particular stage of development, together with the attitudes of the people,
must determine whether collective production can be
introduced without permanently damaging genuine cooperative goals.

This impartial attitude is shared by leading
cooperators in various developing countries who are
aware of the problems and dangers. However, they
dislike to debate these theories unless their specific motives and objectives can be plainly stated.

In 1962, two European authorities with practical
experience in cooperative-collective farming cautiously presented their well-reasoned views against
agricultural collectivism at a meeting of African
cooperators in Berlin (seminar of the German Foundation for Developing Countries). Half of the African
participants expressed strong opposition to the two
principal conclusions of the European speakers. The
Africans disagreed that 1) under normal conditions,
collective farms yield less than the average of individually owned farms, and that 2) collectivism
destroys individualism. The dissenting Africans rejected "dogma" of any kind, and pointed to the success of collective farming in Yugoslavia, Czecho-
slovakia, Israel, and other countries. Also, the
Africans took the same position as some Asian leaders mentioned in the preceding chapter: it is desirable to suppress individualistic tendencies that
hamper social and economic progress.

Views of this kind should not be considered as
mere ideology. In private conversations, the author
discovered that it was not political bias that led
the Africans to defend some experiments of successful
collective farming; rather, it was their basic rejection of dogmatic conclusions. Only positive goals
applied to the specific conditions under which methods
or programs of cooperative-collective actions are to

be performed can be discussed with them in a reasonable manner.

Cultivation of wasteland, irrigation of larger districts, settlement of nomads or formerly landless workers, such structural alterations as the partition of latifundia or the transformation of divided land parcels into economically cultivable farm units--all changes of this nature, which must be initiated under extreme pressure in most developing countries, are not open to considerations other than those of immediate and practical implementation. If the governments, which alone have the power and means to initiate and finance such projects, can find no other solution than collective work, the outcome of the first stages of development must demonstrate the practical results, which, as in the Nawag experiment in Egypt, often lead to adjustments or alteration of a less collective nature.

The choice of a cooperative form of organization for the performance of the type of work described above is to be welcomed, even when the form is not yet adequately filled. It provides the legal basis on which education in discipline and mutual understanding can be built after the most urgent phase of basic technical improvement has been implemented. It is important to remember that tremendous reform programs launched mainly in the agricultural sector usually concern the uneducated masses, and so the leaders find themselves in the tragic dilemma of striving for ends with inappropriate means.

An over-all rejection of cooperative-collective work is unsound in view of the great variety of methods developed along these lines. A representative of the cooperative movement in West Pakistan described the four different types of collective work that agricultural cooperatives perform in his country:

1) Consolidation of small farms through planned cultivation, preservation of the rights of ownership, participation in the returns based on a quota derived from the shares in both land and work.

2)   Genuine collectivism achieved by transferring the ownership rights to the cooperative society,
with completely unified plans of cultivation decided
upon by democratic principles of decision and administration; the members become wage earners, with the
returns dependent upon the size of the originally
owned lots.

3)   Limited collectivism, according to the system
developed by Professor Otto Schiller of Heidelberg
during his stay in Pakistan.   Only the cultivation,
planning, and marketing of products are jointly performed.   Ownership rights, as well as the work itself, remain under the control of the individual members acting on the basis of the common plan.

4)   A combined system of cooperative ownership
and leasehold arrangements; the cooperative society
owns a large area of cultivable land and leases small
sectors to its members, who are pledged to work as
jointly planned but are otherwise independent and
free to use the cooperative facilities of supply and
marketing or to perform these functions alone.

The representative from Pakistan stated that in
his country the fourth system is favored, at least
during the present era of building corresponding
units, and in consideration of the farmers' wishes.
Cultivation and irrigation were often jointly performed in Pakistan before cooperatives were introduced, when large sectors of land were under government administration and new settlers were mere wage
earners.   The old system has been abandoned, and the
government's present policy is to grant a share of
the profits to untrained workers in order to prepare
them for their future status as independent farmers.
The same considerations were responsible for expanding
the use of leasehold arrangements within the framework of cooperatively owned farms.   The member-tenants
may acquire ownership of the leased plots after a
certain period of probation.   The purchase price is
credited over ten to twenty years, and cashed by retaining up to 40 per cent of the annual crop.

A more comprehensible system of collective

farming, recommended by an Indian representative, completely merges neighboring farm lots under a guarantee that every member can, after a specified time, reclaim his holding and return to work on his own.

The Deputy Administrator of the Farmer Cooperative Service of the U.S. Department of Agriculture, Martin A. Abrahamsen, divides the Indian cooperative societies using collective farming methods into four categories:

1) Cooperatives formed for extended production. Ownership and cultivation remain independent. The selection of seeds, use of fertilizers and insecticides, amelioration work, and crop marketing are performed cooperatively.

2) Cooperative ownership of land leased to the members. Work regulations as in (1).

3) Individual land ownership. All operations are cooperatively performed and based on cooperative planning. Earnings are distributed according to a formula based on land ownership and work performance.

4) Totally collective farms. Cooperative ownership of the land and earnings distribution according to work performed.[1]

Mr. Abrahamsen does not evaluate the different types of cooperatives, but a concluding remark points to their insignificant role in the Indian agricultural cooperative movement. They cultivate approximately 80,000 hectares; numerically, they do not exceed 1 per cent of the existing units.

A similar judgment is reached by Dr. H. K. Nook, former chief of the ILO Department for Cooperatives. He concludes that there are 5,600 agricultural cooperatives operating collectively, cultivating 280,000 hectares of land, and accounting for 2.5 per cent of the existing units.[2] Dr. Nook's higher figures still indicate that collective farming in India is kept within small limits. This, however, is only one observation in Dr. Nook's comprehensive international survey. His general conclusion is that, except for Communist countries, cooperative-collective farming methods play a major role in only Egypt, Israel, and other nations where large-scale agrarian reform is taking place. As characteristic of the "ratio" in collective farming, he observes that "the targets of collective farming may often be economically motivated, but more often combined with pseudo-economic motivations of a social, political, or religious character." Dr. Nook points to the Israeli development, where only the first settlers applied total collectivism; the system was modified in later cooperative societies, with more liberal rules to meet consumer needs.

The FAO characterizes collective farming as "a possible solution of the old problem of split land," as "some form of consolidation" is necessary to enable the owners of the smallest holdings to participate in progress.[3] This cautious remark may be the FAO's warning against collective farming except to help owners of split lots acquire economically sound methods of cultivation.

Some detailed comments on productive cooperatives have been made by G. St. Siegens, Director of the Rural Institution and Services Division of the FAO:

> The form of cooperation which seems to be of increasing interest to many developing countries where agrarian reform and settlement programs are under way is that of cooperative farming. The idea of pooling the limited resources of small, uneconomic holdings in order to achieve the advantages of large-scale farming is certainly most appealing. It is for this reason that an increasing number of countries in Asia, Africa and Latin America are planning and implementing projects of this type. While cooperative farms can be established on the basis of free initiative and voluntary support of the farmers themselves, in most cases they are set up, supported, and controlled by governments.

Whether cooperative farming is to be regarded truly cooperative in the Western sense, or as collective enterprise as developed in the socialized world of the East, depends mainly on these factors:

1) degree of voluntariness
2) form of ownership of the production elements
3) responsibility for decision-making

Between the two extremes, varying forms are possible and in fact do exist. It is, therefore, not always easy to draw a clear line between the different forms of cooperative farming. Moreover, the principles of voluntariness, private property, and democratic control may have little significance among peasants who are inadequately prepared either through education, tradition, or experience for the implied responsibilities.[4]

If the above statement is a recommendation for cooperative farming, it is a strongly qualified one. The reader should take into consideration that the FAO's position as a leading international body in agricultural activities compels its representatives to reserved expressions of their eventual criticism. In this light, the above quotation may be regarded as another warning to abstain from cooperative farming except under emergency conditions. But these conditions do prevail in many developing countries, where otherwise inappropriate methods of cooperation are a step in the right direction. It may be no accident that the same issue of the FAO periodical Land Reform, in which the Siegens article appeared, also carries a report of an experiment made in Dahomey. The government chose two areas, one of 600 hectares and another of 4,000 hectares, in which cooperatives of oil cultivation and production were organized. All cultivators in these areas were compelled to join the cooperatives, although they officially retained their ownership rights. The original boundaries of their holdings disappeared during the joint operations. Present membership is open to

landowners as well as landless workers. For every
1½ hectares of land and every 200 days of work performed, one share of the cooperative's stock is
granted to a participant. By retaining three-fifths
of the earned wages, a member accumulates one capital
share over the first 200 workdays. The value of the
land contributed earns 3 per cent interest, and all
working members participate in the net resuts. Management is elected by the members, but two government
representatives must sit on the board of directors.

During the first two years, only one-fifth of
the original program has been completed, i.e., 200
men work in an area of 850 hectares in contrast to
the 1,000 workers and 4,600 hectares envisioned in
the government's plan. Except for some initial difficulty in providing adequate housing for new settlers
in the region, the report does not point to any technical complications experienced during the first
stages of the experiment. The closing sentence of
the article is significant: "But there are the more
difficult problems of adjustment by the people concerned to a system which is novel and complex, and
combines large-scale farming on modern lines, processing of produce, and marketing." In a report that
approves the idea of the project and the organization
of its practical execution, such distinct doubts about
human adaptability to the experiment must certainly
be viewed as a warning against overemphasis on the
technical success of a cooperative experiment that is
particularly inconsistent with the cooperative principles of voluntary membership.

Thus, in collective farming, the psychological
aspects may have an even greater significance than in
other areas. This is the tenor of a short report on
the Cooperative Farming Workshop organized by the
International Cooperative Alliance in Pakistan, in
December, 1962. The conclusions of this body are
more important than the remarks quoted above, because
leaders of several developing countries were at the
workshop, and because its organizing body, the ICA,
includes member countries with collective tendencies
and so cannot be suspected of attempting to propagate traditionalism. The report states:

A Cooperative Farming Workshop was organized by the International Cooperative Alliance (ICA) Education Center in collaboration with the West Pakistan Cooperative Union at Lahore, Pakistan, from 5 to 19 December 1962. It was attended by twenty-three participants from Ceylon, the Federation of Malaya, Thailand, India, and Pakistan. The subjects discussed included the economics of agricultural cooperation, the social and economic benefits of joint farming, limitations of cooperative farming, management and labor organization problems in farming societies, and the organization of technical skills and agricultural facilities. The workshop felt that while cooperative farming would lead to certain economies as regards better utilization of land and other resources, the farm management and labor organization problem in these cooperative societies would be quite complicated. The cooperative farming societies will also have to struggle against certain adverse psychological reactions to proposals of pooling land. On balance, it was felt that cooperative farming cannot be recommended as a national policy of land utilization. The cooperative farming societies may, however, be useful in certain situations, i.e., for bringing new land under cultivation, for rehabilitating certain sectors of the community, and for farmers who cultivate uneconomic holdings.[5]

This conclusion by an assembly of experts, who cannot be accused of prejudice against new methods of cooperation, reflects the main objections that also were expressed in later remarks and reports from nearly all parties involved. The initially mentioned modifications of collective farming methods (quoted from another Pakistan source) show the attention given to avoiding the psychological difficulties of the system without giving up its advantages where the situation requires joint agricultural production. The following observations refer to African countries:

One of the greatest difficulties encountered in the agricultural development in
Africa is to be found in the establishment
of appropriate forms of organization for
agricultural production. The hitherto-
dominating position of privately owned
large-scale farm units will probably dis-
appear despite their economic advantage,
because political and social considerations
are against their continuation. The traditional African family farm, on the other
hand, often does not sufficiently contribute
to economic development. It is for this
reason that many African countries, after
reaching political independence, try to
combine the economic advantages of large-
scale farming with the social advantages
of family farms in the form of cooperative
land cultivation.[6]

The author, Dr. N. J. Newiger, is an expert on
agricultural cooperation in the Rural Institutions
and Services Division of the FAO, Rome, and recently
spent about two years in East Africa, primarily Kenya
and Tanzania. He is also the author of a report on
cooperative farming in Kenya based on an investigation initiated by the Kenya administration and performed by him.[7]

The urgent problem in Kenya was to break up the
large, highly productive farms in the "White Highlands." During the colonial period, this region was
reserved for Europeans only. This, plus the scarcity
of cultivable land in other parts of the country,
understandably created a deep resentment in the natives. The prohibition against their settling in the
White Highlands was the main cause of the Mau Mau
revolts in the 1950's and the ensuing fight for independence, attained in 1963. A program--initiated
by the British prior to independence--to break up
some of the large estates into small farms for landless native peasants was the first project undertaken
by the new government.

In order to preserve the advantages of large-
scale cultivation, the government launched a widespread propaganda campaign to form farm-purchase cooperatives to collect money for the acquisition of
the former European farms. More than 350 such cooperatives were established between 1963 and 1965.
This number far exceeded the expectations of the government, which was in no way prepared for it. The
cooperative department had had no experience except
with already-established forms of agricultural cooperation organized according to British tradition.
About 800 cooperative societies--mainly vegetable-
marketing cooperatives--were registered in 1965. Of
the 1.2 million acres to be sold, 112,000 acres went
to 66 of the 350 new farm-purchase cooperatives by
the end of 1965.

Many of these cooperatives were actually "de-
facto corporations," according to Dr. Newiger's investigation. Their members were government employees,
traders, and businessmen who lived and worked in the
cities and hired managers to run the farms with salaried workers. They had no knowledge of how a cooperative functioned--and no intention to operate that
way--but had chosen the cooperative form only because
registration costs and connected expenses were lower
for cooperatives than for corporations. However,
most of the new cooperatives were formed by landless
peasants or small farm owners who could not participate in the land redistribution except by joining a
cooperative; they had no idea of cooperative principles and their practical application.

Government concern over the unsatisfactory beginnings of the cooperative land-redistribution plan
is reflected in a "manifesto" published by the Republic of Kenya.[8] It declares that all forms of land
ownership shall be put under governmental control,
mainly to prevent any concentration of economic power. Cooperative societies, formed by former workers
and landless peasants, shall have credit and other
privileges. A number of principles stated in the
Newiger report shall be considered in new cooperative
laws, including the request that all members of a
cooperative shall stay on the farm land and participate

in the cultivation; that, except for specialists,
no salaried workers are to be employed permanently,
that members are allowed to reserve a small area for
producing individual family needs, whereas cultivation of products for the market is reserved for collective farming on the larger part of the cooperative
farm; additional regulations based primarily on the
findings of the FAO expert; and, finally, the recognition of the need of strong government control to
avoid abuses and failures in the application of
collective-cooperative farming methods.

The second part of Dr. Newiger's report deals
with the quite different situation in neighboring
Tanzania. There a plan, devised by a team of World
Bank experts, for the reorganization of agriculture
was presented to the government in 1961. Under this
plan, the government expects to establish sixty-nine
cooperative village settlement projects for about
250 families each. Five of these projects were in
existence by the end of 1965. But all were under
immediate governmental control, and had not introduced cooperative methods. Village development committees have been established to prepare and educate
the villagers in all matters concerning cooperation.
The biggest handicap is reported to be the lack of
discipline among the Tanzanian population. In some
settlements, only one-third to one-half of the members come to work regularly, and the settlement leaders are unable to carry out their objectives without
employing salaried workers from neighboring areas.
The lack of discipline is reported to be caused essentially by the collective system itself: the members are accustomed to individual work and do not
understand dividend calculation, which they regard
unjust. Replacement of the collective farming system with cooperative forms of individual land cultivation has been considered. The individually owned
lots would be rearranged in a way making it possible
to apply mechanized tools on large tracts but to
leave all work done by hand to the individual settler
on his own lot.

The report on Kenya and Tanzania is rather discouraging about the results of collective farming.

Dr. Newiger's article summarizes his findings as
follows:

> Both countries are confronted with con-
> siderable difficulties in their new coop-
> erative experimentation, although in dif-
> ferent respects. Kenya does not yet pos-
> sess a sufficient conception of the work
> to be done, and has still to build up an
> appropriate administration for the appli-
> cation of a corresponding plan. Tanzania
> needs more qualified personnel and better
> preparation and operation of most projects.
> They are, in consequence of their prepara-
> tion by unqualified persons and also
> through political influence, often over-
> capitalized and economically unsound. The
> difficulties in both countries are not in-
> surmountable and originate more in inade-
> quate conditions, the improvement of which
> seems to be possible, than in the problem
> of cooperative land cultivation itself
> [translated from German by the author].[9]

A. O. Ellman, the manager of one of the five cooperatively organized settlements established by the
Tanzanian Government and mentioned in Dr. Newiger's
reports as part of the project to establish sixty-
nine village establishments, offers an insignt into
the problems of building a cooperative farming unit
where no other ways of settlement can be found.[10]

Mr. Ellman was assigned by the Tanzanian Government to develop the first settlement under the
program in Kitete, an area in the northern highland
region of the country. The region was virtually un-
occupied for several years after 1961, when the government declared it closed until enough money was
available to finance a cooperative settlement. Several farmers had already moved into the region, but
were not able to develop their farms because of the
hazards of wild game and the danger of attack by
tribes of cattle raiders. Kitete occupies 6,500
acres of land, 5,000 to 6,000 feet above sea level.
The nature of the land and the farming system adopted

make it impossible to divide the area into small holdings. Thus, the whole farm is run as a single unit, owned by the 100 farmers who have formed a cooperative society. Each member contributes his share of the labor requirements and receives a hundredth share of the profits.

The main problem at Kitete has been sociological rather than technical. Mr. Ellman defines the problem as being "to introduce the community feeling and sense of ownership that is essential for the maintenance of enthusiasm, and to effect the strict discipline without which the scheme would collapse." For this purpose, he made it clear to the settlers that "Kitete was their own farm, that as soon as they had paid back to the government the money which they had been loaned, all the equipment, buildings, etc., on the farm would be theirs, and that the harder they worked the greater their profit and the sooner the farm could really be called their own." Furthermore, they were informed that the manager had been put there "in order to ensure that government money was not misused and to train the settlers in the new techniques of agriculture, machinery use, construction, etc. However, he would not stay forever, and the settlers must therefore learn to take responsibility themselves, and the quicker they learned to run the farm themselves the sooner would they be free of external direction."

Mr. Ellman found this approach successful, although there was "no shortage of instances of absenteeism, negligence in performing tasks, etc.," which had to be dealt with by a system of fines. After a short while, however, it was possible to transfer limited authority to elected committees, and a high degree of solidarity was reached. In the first three months, 600 acres of land were cleared and prepared for cultivation. The first crop of wheat was harvested in September, 1964, with a profit of approximately $200 for each settler. In 1965, 1,200 acres of wheat were harvested, plus 300 acres of food crops in the settlers' homestead plots. The farm had begun to pay for itself.

Among the "lessons of Kitete," the following appear to be most remarkable:

The settlers must be farming people, all of one tribe, and should come from the region in which the settlement is located. Cooperative farming is accepted by the people if they realize that there is no workable alternative. Such projects should never be introduced for purely ideological reasons. The settlers must be led to regard the farm as their own property and responsibility. The manager must initially have complete authority, but should adopt the role of teacher rather than dictator, since "in all independent developing countries, any idea of authoritarianism as a long-term policy is politically out of the question."

These conclusions, based on practical work under generally difficult conditions, are dramatic illustrations of how success in cooperative farming depends upon adequate sociological and psychological ways of promotion and management.

The editor-in-chief of the journal Modern Village, Dr. W. Lipski of Warsaw, gives a particularly significant view of the ideological factor in cooperative-collective farming, describing the various methods of "socialist economy in agriculture" applied in Poland and tracing their development up to 1966.[11] His report deals primarily with agricultural producers' cooperatives, although it says that they constitute only "a small part of socialized agriculture in Poland." Until 1956, referred to by Dr. Lipski as the "peak period," more than 10,000 agricultural producer cooperatives existed in Poland. However, these represented only 6 per cent of the individual peasant families, who farmed about 9 per cent of the total arable land. Other forms of cooperation or collective farming, such as the "agricultural circles"; "voluntary universal socioeconomic peasant organizations . . . for the purpose of increasing and improving agricultural production"; and the "peasants' self-aid" cooperatives that farm the land taken over from the State Land Fund, are not included in the following statement regarding Polish

experience with cooperative farming over the last
ten to fifteen years:

> A large number of the cooperatives had been
> set up between 1949 and 1953, a period of
> intense collectivization of peasant farms.
> This process was accompanied by errors in
> agricultural policy--overburdening by taxes
> and quota deliveries, insufficient supplies
> of production means, violation of the volun-
> tary membership principle in setting up agri-
> cultural producers' cooperatives, bureau-
> cratization of agricultural management, and
> underestimation of the importance of self-
> government in peasant dissolution of agri-
> cultural producers' cooperatives in the
> 1956-57 period.

Approximately only 1,000 of the more than 10,000
cooperatives survived the crisis, which ended with
the establishment of a National Council of Producers'
Cooperatives in 1956, followed by the formation of
the Central Union of Producers' Cooperatives in 1962.
Although backed by a resolution by the National Congress of Poland regarding the basic statutory principles of the agricultural producers' cooperatives--
voluntary membership and internal self-government--
the movement did not regain much of its lost momentum
until 1966. A comparison of the years 1956 and 1966
shows the drastically reduced role of producers' cooperatives.

	1956	1966
Number of societies	10,000	1,225
Member families	188,000	22,000
Hectares under cultivation	1,867,000	215,600

The fundamental rules applied in the cooperatives' constitution are:

1) Voluntary membership and unanimously adopted
statutes.

2) The basic share unit is the land contributed.

This remains the shareholder's property, entitling him to an annual rent fixed by the statute, with payment according to the quantity and quality of work done in one working day.

3) Part of the cooperatives' income is transferred to an indivisible fund; the remaining net income is distributed among the members on the basis of workdays performed.

Members can have small plots of their own. These are used mainly for livestock breeding. The size of the plots and the number of livestock is regulated by statute. On the average, the total income of the members breaks down as follows: for work done in the cooperative, two-thirds; for cultivation of privately owned plots, one-third.

The report points out some remarkable forms of state assistance to the producers' cooperatives. For instance, payment of the farm managers' wages from the State Fund (raising the problem of truly independent management); partial financing of cooperative investments by the State Fund; guaranteed credits; tax exemptions; and payment of the members' social insurance cost by the state. These sizable contributions by the Polish Government may indicate its interest in the development of such cooperatives, but they may equally demonstrate the government's intention to retain the control that automatically follows from granting benefits, despite all legal stipulations of autonomy.

A final quote from Dr. Lipski illustrates that even behind the Iron Curtain practicability can overcome ideology:

The greatest progress was achieved in developing those forms of collective farming that do not interfere with the private property of the peasant farmer but are supplementary and auxiliary to individual peasant farming. The main condition of basing cooperation in agriculture on healthy principles is the observance of the principle

of voluntary membership and internal self-
government. . . . Compliance with these
principles may frequently seriously delay
the setting up of the different forms of
cooperative farming and thus hinder modernization and the advance of agriculture. . . .
However, attaining collectivization gradually by convincing the farmers of the need
for it, is, in the long run, by far the most
effective policy.[12]

There is little doubt that these conclusions
comply with the beliefs of most people involved or
interested in cooperative farming, and reflect the
dominant factor of practicability, on which collective production, no less than any other type of cooperative work, depends.

Cooperatives for joint production in areas other
than agriculture are generally less criticized for
being inconsistent with the basic principles of cooperation. They are less exposed to public attention
than all agricultural institutions, and their variety
makes it difficult to form a uniform judgment. Genuine productive cooperatives of workmen in the same
trade who join forces on their own initiative to obtain such benefits as mechanization, financing, marketing, or supply are rare. In developing countries,
cooperative production by artisans is usually found
where traditional handiwork is performed at home.
Other forms of genuine workmen's productive cooperatives belong to "the most difficult tasks of cooperative undertakings," as expressed in a recent ILO report, although the Geneva organization adds that
workmen's productive cooperatives have been established during the last few years in several new
fields--for instance, among printers, shoemakers,
textile workers, homebuilders, and cabinetmakers. It
is too early to report on either their results or the
impact of their methods on the members' individual
and professional well-being.

The Egyptian harbor workers' cooperatives previously described are not really the regular type of
joint-production societies. They are initiated by

forces outside of the directly concerned producers'
group and have followed a course more unionlike than
consistent with joint-production goals.

In contrast to workmen's production cooperatives, the ILO registers craftsmen's cooperatives
established to conserve specific arts and techniques,
i.e., mainly for the professional education of the
young generation of craftsmen. In most cases, this
objective is combined with other purposes of joint
production, so these cooperatives are rightly listed
among production cooperatives. They are found primarily where precision mechanics are well developed.
Since these techniques are rarely applied in developing countries, they may not be of immediate interest
to most of them. However, some examples described
in the foregoing chapter show that similar work can
be performed in the interest of preserving traditional native handiwork and are, as a matter of fact,
applied in various developing countries with considerable success.

The ILO report finally reports various types of
cooperatively organized groups of workers that represent "mixed undertakings," i.e., units established
for joint production but essentially to protect the
workers from the exploitation that they are exposed
to individually. Such cooperative groups work as
subcontractors, and are reported to exist in India,
Ceylon, Israel, and some Latin American countries,
where they work for builders in road construction,
forestry, irrigation, and transportation.

The author did not encounter any basic objections to nonagricultural production cooperatives of
the different types mentioned above, at least not
with regard to the inherent cooperative goals. But
there is a certain reluctance by some leaders in developing countries to promote any kind of cooperation
among the working class. This attitude will probably be emphasized where joint-production tendencies
lead to cooperative formations. These may develop
an even more independent status than other types of
cooperatives, and so are politically suspect by governments that distrust independent organization of
any kind.

NOTES TO CHAPTER 3

1. Martin A. Abrahamsen, A Look at Agricultural Cooperatives in India (Washington, D.C.: Farmer Cooperative Service, U.S. Department of Agriculture, 1961).

2. H. K. Nook, "The Economic and Social Significance of Rural Cooperation" (Second Study Course Paper) (Geneva: ILO, December, 1963).

3. FAO, "Cooperatives and Land Use" ("Development Paper," No. 61) (Rome: FAO, 1962); also FAO memorandum, "Work of FAO to Assist the Development of Cooperatives" (Rome: FAO, August, 1963).

4. G. St. Siegens, "Agricultural Cooperatives and State Sponsorship in Developing Countries," Land Reform (journal of the FAO) (July, 1964).

5. FAO, Land Reform (1963), p. 18.

6. N. J. Newiger, "New Forms of Cooperation in East Africa's Agricultural Production," Zeitschrift fuer das gesamte Genossenschaftswesen (Journal for All Aspects of Cooperation) No. 3 (1966). A more comprehensive report was published by the IFO Institute for Economic Research, Munich, Germany (the co-sponsor of Dr. Newiger's research work) in April, 1967.

7. N. J. Newiger, Cooperative Farming in the Former Scheduled Areas of Kenya (Nairobi: Government of Kenya, Cooperative Department, 1965).

8. Government of Kenya, African Socialism and Its Application for Planning in Kenya (Nairobi: Government Printer, 1965).

9. Newiger, Cooperative Farming in the Former Scheduled Areas of Kenya, op. cit.

10. A. O. Ellman, "A Land Settlement Scheme in Northern Tanzania," Land Reform, No. 1 (1967).

11. W. Lipski, "Forms of Collective Farming in Poland," Land Reform, No. 1 (1967).

12. Ibid.

CHAPTER 4 COOPERATIVE CREDIT AND SAVINGS

A primary motive for establishing cooperatives
in developing countries is the desire to end the exploitation of large parts of both the rural and urban
population by usurious moneylenders. The dual aim
of giving people access to credit facilities at reasonable terms and of inducing otherwise indifferent
and reactionary persons to join cooperatives prompts
governments to channel large funds to the organized
part of the working population mainly through ad hoc
established cooperative units. This inevitable first
step, and the inherent danger of not adhering to the
basic principles of cooperation, have already been
discussed at length. It has been concluded that,
despite these precarious beginnings, deficient cooperatives can be transformed into genuine ones if
there is a will to educate the people toward self-
help, mutual understanding, and trustworthiness. Frequently this will is hampered by a lack of confidence
among native leaders in the spiritual and material
readiness of their people to understand the principles
and ideas--particularly with regard to the financial
implications of self-administered cooperatives. Some
governments attempt to retain their dominant role as
long as possible, and seek to justify continuing the
dependent status of cooperatives. But even without
such interference, it is often difficult to convince
the native leaders of their people's ability to function.

Discovering these abilities, particularly if a
country's backwardness seems to be borne out by sta-
tistical data and facts published by its own government, depends on establishing independent contacts
with the people--unhampered, if possible, by

accompanying officials--and on careful, detailed research. Representative individuals of different social and professional strata who at least know the
needs and potentialities of their neighbors and professional colleagues are the best sources of information. Such an investigation by no means seeks to
undermine a government's policy; on the contrary, it
brings to the leaders' attention facts and potentialities that they often are unable to discover themselves. It must be kept in mind that most leaders
in developing countries work under continuous pressure, combined with ever-present political unrest,
and a lack of well-educated and reliable co-workers
deprives them of information other than the often
superficial and global data of average production,
consumption, and income, which so often distort the
actual situation. Making the leaders aware of the
true facts, without any criticism, is an often gratifying duty of foreign advisers, in the experience
of the author and others who have worked in developing countries.

A typical contrast between conclusions derived
from general information and those obtained by individual observation may be seen in the author's experience after an extended visit to cooperative organizations in a Mediterranean country. Several
months later, he participated in a conference at
which a leading representative of the same country
reported:

> The average income of my country's rural
> population is about $150 per year, but
> nearly 25 per cent of the peasants have an
> average income of $85 only, which latter
> amount is 40 per cent less than what is
> regarded as a minimum income required for
> a family's subsistence in my country. This
> income, which does not even cover current
> expenses, makes it nearly impossible to
> collect any savings and to invest the amounts
> required to develop the agricultural enter-
> prises. It hampers the farmers' producti-
> vity, deprives them from borrowing money
> from nonagricultural sources and opens the

way to all kinds of exploitation by sellers
and buyers.

Listening to this rather hopeless report, the
author remembered the conditions he had found some
months previously, then checked his memory against
the notes brought home from his visit. Some of the
conditions fitted the delegate's over-all picture,
but many were quite different. In a considerable
number of the visited agricultural cooperatives, the
period of initial trouble was over, and some were
even beginning to communicate with neighboring societies, exchange experiences, and, occasionally,
help each other where possible.

The success of most of these societies was due
to a carefully conducted propaganda and education
campaign in credit and saving. Some cooperative
leaders pointed to the modest beginning of capital
accumulation and the improved credit turnover as
evidence of the growing self-help consciousness among
the peasants and villagers. They even complained
that some provisions and controls of the central
authorities were interfering with their proven ability to carry out cooperative self-administration.
This may have been premature, but it certainly was
an indication of the potentialities of cooperative
credit and saving policies even in poor regions, if
the policies are properly prepared and carefully implemented. Such observations should always be
brought to the attention of the highest authorities
involved. They are often useful in helping to get
the officials to abandon certain attitudes caused by
a lack of detailed information.

The prevailing agrarian character of the economy of most developing counries puts the problems of
agricultural credit above all other financial concerns. The common goal is higher production, which
is necessary not only to make more products available
for consumption and export but, even more, to build
up the funds required for investment, i.e., capital
stocks. A vicious circle results because capital is
required to increase production, and higher productivity is the only genuine source of capital

formation and therefore must come first. Credit is
the medium used to solve the problem of increasing
production before the producer disposes of the capital funds required. If credit is properly applied,
the resulting increase in production makes it possible
first to amortize the initial loans, then to build
up capital reserves in the form of reserve funds or
new productive investments. These elementary facts--
but mainly that credit, regardless of the source, is
only a provisional medium to increase production--
are as easily stated in theory as they are difficult
to keep in mind in most developing countries. The
pressure under which systems and organizations must
be developed in order to channel the urgently required
monetary resources into the hands of the acting performers makes it extremely difficult to observe the
basic rules of careful credit administration. This
applies particularly to the widepsread use made of
the cooperative form of credit distribution. In many
newly developing countries, cooperatives are the
media of performing very different tasks in the framework of agricultural programs--all aimed at improving
and expanding production--but they are not always
sufficiently understood in regard to their specific
financial implications, i.e., the different conditions
under which credits granted for various purposes have
to be controlled and administered.

In nearly all developing countries, there are
three main methods to promote agricultural production,
although they often overlap: 1) extending the existing areas of cultivable land, 2) making structural
changes inside the available areas of cultivable land,
3) improving the hitherto-applied methods of cultivating the land. The first two methods are ordinar-
ily initiated, financed, and guided by either the
governments themselves or their authorized agencies.
Their role in the third method depends on the degree
to which rationalization programs have to be applied,
and on the capacity of the rural population to accept
modernization and to learn new methods, which frequently involve more than technicalities and presup-
pose ideological adaptations to new concepts of production, consumption, the market, and work habits.
The applying of cooperative forms of organization to

all these categories is the paramount source of concern with regard to the future of cooperation in developing countries. This applies mainly to the numerous societies that, in so many reports from developing countries, are qualified as mere "money
channels" without performing any of the functions
and responsibilities that belong to the real objectives of credit cooperatives. Progress toward ac-
tivating the functions of this kind of society depends, to a large extent, on the qualifications of
the auditors or supervisors employed by central banks
or other government agencies in charge of credit administration and control. Through them, the system
of centralized credit, which, properly speaking, deprives the local credit societies of independent
actions, fortunately has at its disposal a built-in
antidote against exaggerated centralization. It is
the assigning of the men in charge of enforcing the
observance of all rules and regulations prescribed
by the central agencies and their branches. The offices of the registrars in all parts of India, the
rural branches of the Egyptian Bank of Agriculture,
the Greek Agricultural Bank, and corresponding central agencies in other developing countries employ
the services of trained credit supervisors who are,
in most cases observed by the author, carefully
chosen and educated for this purpose. Although
chiefly trained in government credit and monetary
policies, the supervisors can in time become middle
men between central and local interests. In Greece,
for instance, where credit applications by individual
farmers are based on strict rules and the application
forms are mechanically collected by the credit cooperatives for presentation to the nearest branch of
the Agricultural Bank, these documents are usually
examined by a supervisor and discussed with the cooperative's management before they are sent to the
bank. This gives the supervisor an opportunity to
propose modifications where required, and, frequently,
to take into consideration particular circumstances
that were not foreseen when the application machinery was originally set up. Although such modifications could never supersede the existing regulations,
they often mitigate eventual hardships in special
conditions. The supervisors thus learn to avoid

rigidity where possible, and often side with the cooperative's interests in convincing the central offices of the necessity of deviations from general
rules. Even more important is the effect of the
supervisor's regular contacts with the cooperatives'
officials and the latter's learning to understand
sound credit policies. On nearly every occasion
when the author talked with credit-cooperative officials in the presence of a supervisor, he was surprised by the harmonious atmosphere and often found
the government agent in accord with criticism of the
cooperative's state of dependence.

It is, in this respect, understandable and even
beneficial for governments with established systems
of centralized credit to concentrate their initial
training efforts on building an efficient corps of
cooperative credit supervisors and auditors rather
than primarily training the cooperative members.
Responsible authorities should be warned, however,
not to rely on well-trained supervisors exclusively.

The credit system applied by the Greek Agricultural Bank at the time of the author's visit to Greece
in the early 1960's may be described in detail as an
example of a state bank's function in relation to
credit cooperatives, where the latter are the official
carriers of the credit system without fulfilling its
presuppositions.

Greece's agricultural credit is jointly administered by the Ministry of Agriculture and the Agricultural State Bank. The latter is divided in two
departments--the general department and a special
one for cooperatives. Less than 10 per cent of the
Bank's total assets--about $500 million--is financed
by its share capital, reserve plus deposits, whereas
in excess of 90 per cent is credits granted by the
Bank of Greece, i.e., directly by the state. According to the great majority of the cooperatively organized part of the Greek rural population, the Bank
distributes nearly 90 per cent of its credits through
the cooperative department. The credit volume depends on the amount that the state is able to place
at the Bank department's disposal, regardless of the

cooperative department's (or the cooperatives') requirements.

The Bank department also has the legal authority
to perform the cooperative audits, which are based,
as far as the credit volume for each credit society
is concerned, on a scheme of fixed sums for each of
the main agricultural products per hectare of cultivated land. The credit cooperatives' credit applications must be based on this scheme and are, accord-
ingly, deprived of the means to take into consideration any individual or other qualitative factors.
The Cooperative Department of the Agricultural Bank
recognized that this regulation of credit allocation
prevented cooperative leaders and members from arriving at an appropriate attitude regarding the principles of individual credit distribution. It sponsored
a tentative plan to apply the scheme to each of about
100 cooperative units as a whole, and to allow the
cooperatives' authorities to distribute the total sum
among the members according to individual standards.
At the time of the author's visit to Greek cooperatives, the results of the tentative plan were still
under discussion and were rather differently eval-
uated. However, most critics agreed that the plan
would be a step in the right direction if carried out
properly. The pros and cons expressed regarding the
ability of most cooperative managements to use the
right to administer credit internally at their own
discretion, avoiding arbitrary judgments and favoritism, were characteristic of the conflict between
the cooperative form and the fiscal method of credit
policies found in most developing countries.

Often, the individual experience of leading officials decides their attitude toward cooperative
liberties. The chief of the Agricultural Bank's cooperative department, who had been educated in a
Western European country, favored self-administration
and proposed trying out the tentative plan on a larger
scale, i.e., extending it to 500 cooperatives. But
strong opposition to any further experiment was expressed by the leadership of the Central Association
of Cooperative Unions, who had a predominantly fiscal
background and a more or less skeptical view of the

Greek peasant's capacity to make sound decisions. Such contrasting views may be found in many countries and cannot be reconciled by persuasion alone. The evidence of the local societies' growing maturity, attained through careful education, is the only proof that will convince skeptics of the cooperatives' capacity for self-administration.

The Greek system just described applies to credits granted for regular purposes only, i.e., for financing the peasants' current work, and not for ameliorations, new settlements, and other activities that belong to the first two categories listed above. Where governments organize such programs, they generally establish special administrations to finance the work, even where it is being performed by ad hoc cooperative societies and the invested funds are officially granted in credit form. This, for instance, is the case in Iran and Egypt.

The land-distribution organization in Iran has its own financial administration, set up by the Shah to take care of the new settlements and the connected cooperatives, and is completely separate from the country's agricultural bank, which deals only with the reorganization and promotion of the cooperatives of already established farmers. The Shah has no influence on the bank's credit and other policies. It seeks to consolidate the cooperative credit system by certain regulations concerning measurement and control. The total credit to be granted to a cooperative society shall not exceed a certain multiple of the paid-in share capital plus reserves. In addition, the bank guarantees, under certain circumstances, the cooperatives' saving deposits and so contributes to the societies' saving campaigns. These campaigns are particularly hampered in Iran by the population's lack of confidence in local institutions.

The Egyptian Land Reform Law of 1952 states in Article 19 the functions of agricultural cooperatives in general, and in a later article decrees that land-reform cooperatives shall be supervised by the government. This does not exclude state control of all other cooperatives, but it does indicate the special

status of land-reform cooperatives in relation to
the government. Up to the present, the trend to intensify state control of all cooperatives seems to
be stronger than reverse tendencies. This trend is
particularly true of credit cooperatives, because of
the disappointing results of autonomous credit management at the expense of the Egyptian State Bank of
Agriculture.

Credit to land-reform cooperatives has been
based on instructions issued by the competent government agency, i.e., without the Bank's controlling influence, whereas the Bank's credit policies concerning other agricultural cooperatives have been directed
toward the development of management's self-
administrative qualifications and growing consciousness of the responsibilities involved. This policy
was required by a new rule, established after the reform of the Egyptian administration, to abandon the
old system of granting credit according to the value
of the debtor's real securities only, and to recognize
instead the farmers' credit requirements as the basic
criterion of credit allocation. This change was made
to eliminate the former advantages of the large estate
owners. The presumption, however, that enough qualified members of cooperative administrations were
available to manage the new system proved to be an
illusion. The Bank of Agriculture was, and still is,
bound to use its branches in all parts of the country
to administer and control cooperative credits, plus
their distribution to and employment by individual
members.

Another defeat in the cooperative structure of
the Egyptian credit system occurred when all banks
and insurance companies were nationalized in 1961,
and private partnership in all such institutions was
prohibited. The name Agricultural Bank of Egypt,
which had been changed to the Agricultural and Cooperative Credit Bank when the cooperative movement
was in its first stage of development, was reinstated,
and a considerable number of the Bank's shares, which
had been sold to cooperative societies as the beginning of future total ownership of the Bank's capital
by the cooperative movement, had to be redeemed. The

nationalization law not only prohibited the sale of
additional shares to cooperatives, but forced the
redemption of shares already sold. Besides the financial implications, the moral effect of the trans-
action was rather depressing, particularly to advanced elements in the cooperative movement. They
were disappointed in their attempts to attain a more
independent status with the increasing transfer of
bank shares to cooperative societies, and at the
same time to rid themselves of the permanent control
exercised by the Bank and its branch agents. The
above-mentioned expansion of the Bank's net of
branches exposed the cooperatives to even closer supervision.

The president of the Egyptian Agricultural Bank
personally expressed to the author his earnest regret
about the decline of cooperative credit administration in his country. Some of the president's information gave the author his deepest insight into the
problems of building a cooperative credit system.

Originally, the educational campaign to establish credit cooperatives in as many rural districts
as possible was performed under the slogan, "Bring
the Bank to the Village." The idea was to end the
peasants' practice of borrowing money from the moneylenders in their villages. The peasants used these
lenders to avoid the inconvenience of traveling to
the nearest branch of the Agricultural Bank. Only
one office was functioning in each larger district
at the time of the campaign. The advantage of the
money's being attainable locally outweighed the
heavy disadvantage of disastrous lending terms. The
establishment of cashier offices in the villages as
subbranches of the Bank, where the members could
have immediate access to cash, was prevented by the
lack of safekeeping facilities in the villages and
also by the peasants' distrust of their neighbors.
At the time of the interview, early in 1962, the
president's estimate of the time required to "bring
the bank to the village" was "at least five additional years," and this was after nearly ten years of
trying to build a workable cooperative credit system.
This illustrates how much patience is required to

achieve a genuinely cooperative-minded credit organization, even in a country like Egypt. Over the
first decade after the revolution, the loans granted
to agriculture were increased to nearly 250 per cent
of the pre-revolutionary average, and since 1961, all
loans have been formally issued as "cooperative
credit."

The slow progress is partly due to the combination of supply and marketing functions with the
credit business, i.e., the building of multipurpose
cooperatives, as is the practice in many developing
countries. Although not undisputed, the multipurpose
society is seen by most experienced advisers to developing countries as a useful and sometimes inevitable form of organizing cooperative credit systems.
It presupposes considerably greater efforts, mater-
ially and educationally, and so involves much more
preparation, investment, and training than cooperatives concerned with credit only. However, combining credit with supply and marketing is unavoidable
where loans and refunds are essentially given and
taken in natural form. This is required by the widespread inexperience among rural populations, as well
as by the need to control the use made of credits
granted for specific objectives.

The Agricultural Bank of Egypt grants most of
its credits by supplying the borrowers with fertilizers, insecticides, and other agricultural needs.
In this way, the Bank is assured that these items
are actually applied by the farmers, and that they
arrive at the farms in good condition. Cotton is
the main cash crop of Egypt, and the Bank, as the
official cotton collector for the government, has at
its branches disposal warehouses, cleaning equipment,
installations for sorting and packing, and trained
workers and employees to guarantee cotton deliveries
as required internationally.

In view of the importance of cotton exports to
Egypt's economy, the centralization of the above
functions is paramount and automatically leads to
acceptance of cotton by the Bank's branches as credit
refunds. These circumstances also discourage

"bringing the bank to the village." If it is not yet possible to install safe cash installations in the villages, as demonstrated by the Bank's president, it is certainly unthinkable to equip village cooperatives with all the material and personnel necessary to collect, clean, sort, and pack cotton as required to sustain the country's export market. This is a temporary situation only, and peculiar to the unique character of cotton in Egypt's economy. The underlying need to grant loans in kind in order to make sure that the farmers get the right things under reasonable conditions, and the likewise important control of the farmers' seasonal income to be used primarily to amortize the loans, argue in favor of combining credit, supply, and marketing in other countries also.

Like Egyptian cotton, various agricultural products represent the economic lifeblood of many developing countries. The competitive world market compels them to make extraordinary efforts in order to meet high requirements for quality, assortment, and packing, which are expected to accommodate the importers' particular methods of mass production and distribution. Failure to satisfy the importers' demands leads to heavy losses, as recently seen in a report from Turkey.[1] Turkish tea exports realize three to four Turkish pounds per kilo, despite a world market price of ten to fourteen pounds for corresponding qualities. Lack of adequate storage facilities and defective sorting and packing accounted for the loss of about two-thirds of the regular price. In order to make good the export losses, the official price is fixed at twenty pounds per kilo of the same quality of tea for the home consumer.

Formerly, private traders, mainly foreign exporters, took care of the processing, packing, and shipping requirements of the export business. But the notorious exploitation by businessmen who shamelessly underpaid the producers had to be abolished. Most new governments were confronted with two alternatives. They could organize and train groups of producers in processing and related export operations that individual producers cannot perform alone, or

they could take over the whole process. The first
alternative was impractical, since too many preparations are required where immediate steps were necessary to carry on the existing export business. The
second alternative presupposes government regulations
to obtain and control products and the establishment
of a state monopoly for their export. These regulations are generally not expected by the peasants and
other producers because of their country's liberation
from "colonial domination," and particular incentives
had to be introduced in order to break resistance
against the export monopoly.

The key to solving this unpopular problem is
credit. As in the cases mentioned in the previous
chapter where the promise of credit was the main de-
vice used in forming cooperative societies, the as-
surance of advance payment for all deliveries to the
export agency makes adherence attractive to producers
who usually object to restrictions of this kind. As
an additional incentive, some governments promise to
transform the export agencies into self-governing
bodies of contributors, and to pave the way for a
future cooperative society of the respective organizations by taking immediate steps to train workers
and employees in all techniques connected with the
export business. This training includes the special
education required for cooperative credit administration under the multipurpose system. The more progress made in combining the credit, supply, and marketing functions, the better are the prospects of
capital formation by means of retained earnings. As
soon as satisfactory export (or other marketing) results are attained, the members should agree to regular deductions from their share of the sale proceeds
to build up share capital. The frequently heard
argument that such deductions will not be accepted
and will reduce membership, has been proved to be
invalid, where the leaders are sincere adherents of
self-administration, unhampered by political considerations and familiar with their members' situations.
A certain flexibility is advisable in particular
cases, where a rigid policy of retained earnings
would lead to hardships and create opposition. Once
the retained-earnings method has built up the members'

capital shares, it can easily be carried on to accumulate regular savings deposits. It is the most
practicable way of inducing savings in even the most
inexperienced members of a cooperative.

The cooperative credit system of India is based
on the government's principle of centralization. But
the enormous size of the country and the great variety of its population are reflected in certain regional deviations from the planned uniformity and in
considerable tendencies toward emancipation from governmental regulations.

The State Reserve Bank of India is the main
source of credit and distributes the available amounts
through twenty-two Cooperative Banks. Half of the
capital of these banks is owned by the governments
of the individual Indian states where they are sit-
uated. Still, there are more than 400 Central Cooperative Credit Banks in operation all over India;
these are genuine cooperative organizations, with an
average of only 20 per cent of their capital owned
by government agencies. The twenty-two Cooperative
Banks function as apex banks in relation to the Central Cooperative Banks in their respective regions.
A peculiar relationship between the local cooperative
banks and their own central banks prevailed until
recently, in that the non-publicly owned 80 per cent
of their capital was (and partly still is) in "private" hands. Most of these "private" shareholders
are members of local cooperatives. They contribute
to these the minimum required to make use of the
cooperative supply, marketing, and other service facilities. Their membership in the central cooperative banks reflects a lack of confidence in the financial reliability of the village cooperatives.
They prefer to handle all monetary operations, credit
as well as saving, directly with the central banks.
Efforts are being made to induce the local cooperatives to expel the "private" shareholders and prohibit them from direct participation in the central
cooperative banks. This policy is being combined
with a general campaign to strengthen the villagers'
confidence in their own local savings institutions.
An average of only 6 per cent of the working capital

of India's cooperatives consists of savings deposits, and plans are being made to at least double this amount through all means of an appropriate savings campaign.

The above data stem from the report of an Indian registrar to the 1960 Cooperative Seminar of the German Foundation for Developing Countries in Berlin. The over-all character of the report neglects certain developments and facts that would be unlikely to appear in a general survey. The individualism exhibited by large sections of India's agricultural and industrial population is reflected in the following accounts presented by some leading experts after recent visits to Indian cooperative organizations. The tendencies against centralism and government dependence, which the registrar's report did not mention, are vital elements of India's cooperative movement, especially its credit organization. The establishment of an Indian organization to privately finance cooperative societies has already been referred to in the report by John M. Eklund.

Additional information is contained in a special report by Martin A. Abrahamsen, Director of the Farmer Cooperative Service of the U.S. Department of Agriculture.[2] He describes the different types of cooperatives in India and details their financial resources. Apart from societies that fully depend on the district banks--on funds provided by the government through the Reserve Bank of India--there are numerous others that mobilize local savings in order to attain as much financial independence as possible. Mr. Abrahamsen states that other credit cooperatives are trying to become independent from the government through foreign-aid funds, and also are campaigning for local contributions in order to prove to the representatives of foreign-aid organizations that their self-help efforts are genuine.

The former president of the Cooperative League of the U.S.A., Jerry Voorhis, reported in a lecture before the American Institute of Cooperation in August, 1964, on a conference attended by the regional leaders of a group of Production Credit Cooperatives in India that he had joined in the fall of 1963. The group, established with initial loans from American organizations several years ago, granted credit to specific types of producers after careful consideration of their individual needs. Delegates from twenty-three different types of societies were present at the meeting, including cooperatives of rug knitters, spice producers and dealers, poultry farmers, plus irrigation, marketing, and general credit institutions. Producers of a particular type are generally granted credit according to their main supply requirements. Membership is based on professional homogeneity. Farmers with less than two or more than six acres of land are not admitted. The cooperative control is mainly directed toward ascertaining that the loans are adequately used for productive ends, but partly concerns the producers' future plans, without infringing on the rights and responsibilities of ownership. Farmers and artisans who are heavily in debt but whose character and performance make them acceptable to a cooperative are eligible for membership in order to help them discharge their debts and raise their productivity and morale as members of a self-help institution. Since cooperative interest rates are lower than those of private lenders, considerable savings result in the debtors' redemption of private loans. The cooperative leaders reported to President Voorhis that they manage, in most cases of this kind, to collect the equivalent of the saved interest margins as savings of the new members. President Voorhis stated that the main objective of the Indian Production Credit Cooperatives was to raise production, and that continuing education in discipline and self-reliance, as practiced by the societies under review, has increased by 20 per cent the productivity of most member operations. Corresponding to the increasing revenue, loan funds are carefully surveyed. The refunds are used to build up revolving funds in the amounts of the initial funds granted by American organizations and left to the permanent disposal of the Indian group. The revolving fund accumulated by one agricultural subgroup has already enabled its leaders to decline additional help offered by their American supporters.

Despite these gratifying results, they indicate
only the beginnings of sound cooperative credit policies in India. The report of the Farmer Cooperative
Service of the U.S. Department of Agriculture quoted
above also states that, at most, 5 per cent of agricultural credit is controlled by India's cooperatives.
This does not mean that the remaining 95 per cent is
left to private moneylenders, since the Reserve Bank
of India also distributes considerable amounts to the
agrarian population through other agencies besides
cooperative banks, but it is generally felt that the
usurers still dominate a very large sector of India's
agricultural credit system. This may still be the
case in most developing countries; at least, it was
until recently. According to a statement issued by
a representative of Thailand in 1960, for instance,
90 per cent of the agrarian credit in his country
was provided by private lenders, and not more than
8 per cent of the rural population belonged to the
country's cooperative movement.

At this point, some comments are relevant on
the terrifying phenomenon of the moneylender, who
plagues nearly all developing countries. It is first
necessary to eliminate certain vague ideas on the
origin and essence of usury and similar exploitation
that are often heard but do not fully explain the
nature of the problem.

The intrinsic nature of an evil as lasting and
widespread as usury, which during the course of history has affected every country in the world, cannot
be determined by an investigation limited to specific
persons and their actions. To condemn them for lack
of a social or moral conscience is of course justifi-
able. But they are mere agents of a system; a system characterized by a deficient social and economic
order. The recognition and understanding of the de-
ficiency, not merely its profiteers, must be the object of an investigation into the genuine origin of
usury.

The ILO report on "The Role of Cooperatives in
the Economic and Social Development of Developing
Countries" singles out the abolition of usury, as

"perhaps the most important role which cooperation can perform," and concludes that "the merchant-moneylender does in fact fulfill indispensable economic functions although at an inadmissibly high price. The need is for some way of fulfilling these functions while avoiding the exploitation of the primary producer." The merchant-moneylender's functions are "indispensable" only if the economic structure of a community fails to provide for their fulfillment through regular financial and commercial establishments. The ILO statement recognizes the often overlooked sociological fact that usury is primarily caused by deficiencies in the economic order of a community.

Where the functional mechanism of an economic structure is incomplete, a vacuum occurs that somehow must be filled, if not by appropriate means, then inevitably by reckless opportunists. Frequently, the vacuum is caused by the risks involved in lending money to people who do not have a real sense of its value or market products of irregular quality. Such risks deter regular bankers and traders. From this point of view, the merchant-moneylenders' rates, prices, and terms are their protection against expected losses—a kind of risk premium that they are able to impose recklessly as long as their monopoly is not broken by structural improvements in the economic community.

The author's explanation of the socioeconomic conditions that bring about exploitation should not be misinterpreted as a moral defense of usury, but should be understood as an attempt to indicate that the evil cannot be erased without eliminating its sources.

A clear recognition of the economic circumstances described is particularly necessary because of the political misuse made of the alleged exploitation by foreigners or past colonial regimes. This charge of foreign exploitation is often used to bring about radical reforms of new governments and to arouse nationalistic feelings in often indifferent masses of natives. It should not be allowed to obscure the true origin of usury--at least in the eyes of leading reformers of the economic and social conditions in a developing country.

The preponderance of private moneylenders in many developing countries, as illustrated by the Indian and Thailand data, is no reason to regard their diminishing influence as a utopian goal. The results already attained by some credit cooperatives are proof that a well-organized cooperative unit can enforce normal credit conditions in large districts. Traders and moneylenders in numerous developing countries soon became aware of the potential influence of a sound lending policy, which appropriate institutions, mainly credit cooperatives, would introduce. They often reacted quickly; in some instances it was even necessary to prevent them from intruding into cooperative establishments, where their still existing influence and considerable authority could outweigh the benefits of cooperation.

Tight controls by governments may, in most instances, prevent private profiteers from interfering with cooperative work, but this control itself is objectionable, at least in the long run. Moreover, no government has at its disposal enough money to cover all credit requirements. The danger of the moneylenders' return is a lasting problem, even where credit cooperatives have initially succeeded in displacing them, if credit and saving are not tied together by institutional and educational provisions. This problem has been recognized in various countries. The following statements show the diversity of individual factors that must be taken into consideration.

Members of credit cooperatives in Thailand are bound, by government decree, to deposit at least 5 per cent of their credit requirements or to agree to a 5 per cent deduction from all loan disbursements. These deductions are credited to a savings account, which cannot be withdrawn as long as the loan is due or before five years have passed. Credit cooperatives were originally established in Thailand after World War I, when the country's rice production could not satisfy the growing demand from abroad. The

peasants' lack of cash made it necessary to develop
a credit system to finance the investments required
to increase production. Stringent rules were established for _ad hoc_ village units to admit as members
and grant credit to only those villagers who agreed
to an unlimited guarantee by each member for the
unit's debts. According to two separate reports
from cooperators from Thailand--the first in Summer,
1960, to an international cooperative seminar in Berlin; the second to the Spring, 1964, term of the International Cooperative Training Center, University
of Wisconsin, Madison, Wisconsin--the severity of
these conditions was, for quite a while, a restraint
to the development of credit cooperatives.

New societies were not established until the
1930's, and received their main stimulus when a Cooperative Central Bank was established in 1943. Most
of the Bank's funds stem from local credit cooperatives, which are under obligation to deposit the
above-mentioned compulsory savings of their members
with the Central Bank. In 1962, the Bank had at its
disposal an operating capital in excess of $15 mil-
lion. A law prohibits dividend disbursements of more
than 10 per cent of net surplus to membership shareholders. This compulsory addition of 90 per cent of
net earnings to the reserve accounts steadily increases the credit cooperatives' capital funds and,
therefore, their independence. The local societies
are allowed to charge their members 10 per cent interest on loans granted by the Central Bank, which
charges the societies only 7 per cent. The 3 per
cent margin is a secure source of regular surplus
and represents an additional element of compulsory
savings for the benefit of Thailand's credit system.

The 10 per cent interest charged to the usually
poor cooperative members is extraordinarily high
compared with cooperative credit terms in Western
countries. However, interest rates must be judged
according to individual market conditions. Appropriate rates are significant components of sound
credit policies, particularly in developing countries,
where a great part of the population is financially
inexperienced. Interest rates that are too low lead

to exaggerated demands for credit. This also results when governments reduce or even eliminate interest charges during emergencies, despite the usual announcement that the move is temporary. In the early 1960's, several years of poor cotton harvest prompted the Egyptian Government to declare a general moratorium on agricultural debts and to cancel "temporarily" all interest charges. The moratorium was intended to grant the credit cooperatives and their members sufficient time in which to make up losses, but instead caused an extraordinary upsurge in requests for credit. In an interview with the author, the management of the Egyptian State Bank of Agriculture expressed mixed feelings regarding the credit concessions. They said that it destroyed the people's understanding of normal credit conditions and reduced all efforts to accumulate cooperative-owned capital funds. They thought that an early end to the moratorium was necessary, but expressed little hope for it because of political considerations that had also prompted the government to issue the moratorium. Such controversial moves by economic and political leaders, drastically affecting credit policies, are problems arising from a government's dominance of the banking system, whether cooperatively or otherwise organized.

A system of combined credit and savings policies, similar to that in Thailand, prevails in neighboring Burma. This may be because the countries have similar economic structures and are in geographical proximity. A particularly successful case of building savings and credit institutions--by the daily setting aside at each family meal of small portions of rice, which are then collected and supervised by a nearby cooperative--in one of the poorest regions of Burma has been referred to earlier in this book. Savings on a larger scale are achieved in Burma by compulsory deliveries of the debtor's crop to the cooperative societies that have granted credit. An agreed-upon part of the crop's value is thereby credited to the supplier's savings account; most of it is used to reduce the unpaid loan balance. This method was first tried in the sugar-cane regions of Burma, and this led to the early development of multipurpose cooperative societies. By 1960, more than 7,400 such

cooperatives were established, all with limited liability. Only about 4,200 were reported as "active"
units. The high percentage of inactive societies
seems to be a consequence of the State Bank's stip-
ulation that it will grant credit to registered cooperatives only. In order to register, a cooperative
must prove that at least 75 per cent of its members
are farmers, and that at least 1 per cent of the required credit is deposited in savings accounts. Often
these conditions can be met only after a cooperative
has been established for some time.

The People's Bank of Indonesia (Indonesia is a
country with decided tendencies toward state socialism) has established an even stronger savings system.
In order to register, a cooperative's officer must
accept the system.[3]

Starting from the smallest collections, as little as five to ten cents per day, more than $22 mil-
lion has been accumulated in about 10,000 cooperatives. Four different types of deposits were established and led to this accomplishment: 1) initial
deposits according to individual regulations, which
must be included in the statutes of each cooperative,
2) equally determined deposits in a fixed relation
to the members' credit claims, 3) additional voluntary savings deposits, and 4) planned savings for
special purposes. The share of each of the four different categories of savings in the total of $22 mil-
lion was as follows:

Initial deposits	$2	million
Fixed deposits	$8	million
Voluntary deposits	$4.25	million
Special deposits	$7.75	million
	$22	million

The high amount for special purposes represents
money reserved mostly for festivities and pilgrim-
ages, rather than for professional or domestic investments. These nonproductive expenditures are an
important element in the people's spending habits in
most developing countries and represent a heavy burden to all credit institutions. It is not possible,

however, to restrict cooperative credit in developing
countries to productive aims as in Western countries,
because certain expenses are so deeply rooted in religious and other traditions. Even the poorest spend
large sums for such ends without incurring criticism
for extravagance. It is part of their life style to
celebrate births, weddings, and funerals with numerous guests and generous hospitality. This socially
unavoidable spending is often the beginning of indebtedness to usurers, who are always ready to lend
money for such purposes. By separating savings for
special purposes from other types of deposits, the
method used in Indonesia draws a clear line between
productive and nonproductive expenditures--the former
qualifying for credit, the latter to be covered by
accumulated savings, as far as possible. This dif-
ferentiation is a valuable contribution to a better
understanding of financial matters by inexperienced
natives; also, it helps to discharge the credit requirements.

Expenditures for ritual and other traditional
purposes, particularly family celebrations, are emphasized in nearly all reports from countries with
predominantly non-Christian populations. The ILO,
AID, the Alliance for Progress, and other agencies
have repeatedly expressed concern over this financial
burden. It is the genuine source of indebtedness in
many regions where cash is required for extraordinary
purposes only and most current obligations are met by
compensation in kind.

Credit cooperatives should adopt the Indonesia
example or similarly appropriate methods wherever
such conditions prevail. American and European observers of aid to developing countries have repeatedly expressed concern over the widespread lack of understanding of the actual obligations and responsibilities involved in receiving and using borrowed
money. Its genuine character as an advance payment
in anticipation of an equivalent return is often not
recognized. Instead of diminishing, this lack of understanding has grown in recent years due to the large
sums pumped by the governments of various developing
countries into often unprepared credit organizations.

Economic and political reasons often leave administrations of newly emerging communities no alternative but to grant monetary help as quickly and amply as possible in order to avoid a complete deadlock in the country's economy and to strengthen the people's confidence in the new course. This, however, causes the above-mentioned danger of distorting the psychological reaction of the recipients of monetary help and damaging the sociological impact on any established order of organized credit, whether in a cooperative or other form. In the face of these dangers, the CUNA system, which builds up small local units of savings and credit associations, has to be pointed up as a proved counterbalance.

The encouraging examples of some governmental and other credit administrations that try to avoid unsound financial-aid transactions should not conceal the ever-present hazards of credit policies that still prevail in these regions. More examples of successful credit policies are given in the ensuing paragraphs in order to show an awareness by many native leaders of the problems involved and to avoid giving the impression that workable ways of recovery cannot always be found.

Groups of cooperative societies in both parts of Pakistan succeeded in accumulating capital for special purposes under a well-organized system. About 10,000 refugees were settled in more than 100 cooperatives in West Pakistan. The government made cultivable land available to leaseholders, who later were allowed to buy their lots. Cooperatively organized, the settlers increased their own payments of share capital from $4,000 in 1948 to $115,000 in 1959 and, over the same span of time, set aside an additional $100,000 in savings--a total accumulation in excess of $20 for each settler, from the net income of the rented farms over and above all expenses, originally financed exclusively by credit.[4]

The East Pakistan experiment of a regional academy for village development in and around Comilla

was based on careful studies of the potential means
of cooperation in the district, including the acti-
vation of the until then inefficient operations of
a number of cooperatives. Credit and saving were
combined through a district center, to which the cooperatives were admitted after a probationary period
of four to six months, during which they agreed to
collect savings according to an individualized schedule. Warehouse facilities were installed to enable
the cooperatives to both collect the crops and further savings accumulations. At the time of delivery,
60 per cent of the crop value was advanced to the
suppliers. Considerable profits were realized by
storing the delivered goods until after the harvest,
when prices usually rise about 40 per cent. The realized profits were split in three parts--one added
to the cooperative's reserves, one paid out to the
members, and the last credited to the respective
members' savings accounts.

The results achieved in both East Pakistan and
West Pakistan were based on the most careful investigations of the needs and potentialities of the local population. Strong discipline and centralized
controls were unavoidable in both cases. But these
controls were ordered not by distant government
agencies but by regional authorities, who closely
observed the district's social and human reactions.

All the above experiences took place in countries
with ancient cultural traditions, which, in spite of
their technical and organizational deficiencies, often provide serviceable foundations for a new order.
For instance, there are the ancient village institutions of mutual help, the widespread concept of family solidarity, the many tribal traditions, all of
which can eventually be mobilized in the interest of
new beginnings, particularly in cooperatives. In
larger regions of Africa, mainly south of the Sahara,
less favorable conditions prevail. At the same time,
the political unrest in many Middle and South African
countries is more disturbing than in other developing
areas, so that the governments are forced to spend
more of their material and personal resources, as
well as time, on political and military rather than

social and cultural objectives. Furthermore, the
resentment against the only recently abolished colonial administrations is generally stronger in these
countries than elsewhere.

All these factors--the absence of renewable
cultural traditions, the political preoccupation of
the leaders, and the fresh memories of "colonial exploitation"--are obstacles to sound financial policies, particularly to the introduction of cooperative
credit and savings methods. Similar institutions
from colonial times, such as the Sociétés de Prévoyance, have, for the most part, been abolished and
discredited. There is a general abhorrence of any
compulsory form of building up reserves in either
kind or money. Although occasional exceptions appear
in many African nations (for example, those mentioned
by Director Waidelich of the cooperative school in
Stuttgart-Hohenheim, Germany, in his report of a
visit to Nigeria in 1963), the general prospects for
progress are less promising than elsewhere.

The exceptional conditions in Nigeria may be explained by the fact that this country was under British administration until independence was achieved,
and thus had less resentment of the colonial regime
and its institutions than those countries under Belgian or French administration. Favorable impressions
of Nigeria's prospects for sound credit policies
appear in the report of a study tour of AID and CUNA
experts through various African countries during the
first half of 1964. The tour was specifically directed toward assessing the chances for building up
credit unions in the regions visited. The principal
conclusions of the report give an extraordinarily
precise picture of the outlook for credit and savings
projects already under way in the areas under observation.[5]

1) Sudan. No firm bases on which to build cooperatives have been found, but some leaders have
recognized the "considerable influence on the social,
financial, and general welfare of the people" that
a cooperative credit program would exert in view of
the lack of education and confidence of most natives.

Tribal chiefs of two regions of Sudan have applied
to the government for help in establishing credit
cooperatives, teachers, military personnel and employees, each in a specific cooperative establishment
and utilizing their respective professional bodies.

2) <u>Ethiopia</u>. Some credit unions for government
officials are in operation, but there appears to be
no initiative to organize a large-scale credit cooperative movement. Marketing is the only cooperative
area in agriculture. Credit and savings cooperatives
were not expected to be established without the assignment of foreign experts to work in Ethiopia.

3) <u>Sierra Leone</u>. More than 700 cooperative societies of various types, including credit cooperatives, were reported. But none is active in promoting capital accumulation. The majority of the population is illiterate and suspicious, and most of
the more than 100 officials of the country's Department of Commerce in charge of cooperatives are too
busy with bookkeeping to assist in more essential
cooperative activities. All government representatives were in favor of promoting genuine cooperatives,
and decided in 1964 to send qualified officials to
cooperative schools in the U.S. and Nigeria.

4) <u>Senegal</u>. A number of Peace Corps volunteers
were actively working toward future cooperative initiatives. Their activities, plus strongly organized
tribal associations found in some rural districts of
the country, are a promising sign for the establishment of credit unions. But before this can happen,
a government law requiring deposits to be placed in
privately owned banks only must be abolished.

5) <u>Nigeria</u>. This country offers the best possibilities for credit cooperatives, according to the
report. However, visits to more than 300 cooperative
societies revealed low rates of capital accumulation
due to insufficient promotion and education for saving. The government concedes that strong moves are
required to propagate cooperative credit and savings
methods, mainly to counter the still predominant influence of private moneylenders and traders. A

cooperative school in Nigeria was planning to add
courses for leaders of credit cooperatives, geared
to American standards. The American delegation concluded that the government could achieve its goals
for the development of a credit-cooperative move-
ment--the establishment of 4,000 societies with more
than 400,000 members and close to $10 million in
savings--in the framework of its five-year plan.

6) Tunisia. A small number of credit cooperatives were in existence at the time of the inspection
tour. They had been established recently, since the
government began to promote savings and credit policies. Formerly, only agricultural-supply and marketing cooperatives were in operation. The Tunisian
cooperative school, established under the French administration, was expected to expand to include savings and credit matters. A government program to
raise $2 million in savings over a five-year period
seemed to be not unrealistic.

Despite the variety of the AID/CUNA group's
findings in the African countries, the report comes
to a general conclusion, reflecting the CUNA over-all
concept that organized savings and credit proceedings
are basic prerequisites to cooperative developments
in general. The report states that savings and loan
associations are required to complement other types
of cooperative societies, enabling the members to
pay for their shares as participants in the marketing,
consumer, electricity, handicraft, or other cooperative
institutions they may choose. Moreover, it is generally conceded that large unemployed capital resources are kept by most African populations, and
these must be seen as a stimulus to mobilize the idle
values for productive aims by making available solid
savings and loan institutions. They would, in this
way, most effectively contribute to the economic
progress of Africa's developing countries.

Since this study, the CUNA work has been continued with great success in more than a dozen developing countries. Testimony by leading CUNA officials during hearings on the Foreign Assistance Act
(May, 1967, House of Representatives Committee on

Foreign Affairs; June, 1967, Senate Foreign Relations
Committee) led to unanimous declaration of appreciation from the chairman and various members of the two
committees. [6]

Reports on the combined work of CUNA, AID, and
the Peace Corps[7] illustrate the immediate impact of
CUNA-type credit unions on the community life of a
whole region. Two examples only may be cited, both
from South American regions.

According to the AID report, the very poor population of the city of Iquitos in Peru, in an isolated
jungle region on the Amazon River, has experienced
the gratifying influence of credit-union work on the
whole community. This occurred in less than four
years. Organized in the poorest district of the city,
the credit union became the largest of its type in
Peru. With 3,500 members and about $750,000 in de-
posits, it began to further the city's construction
work by financing the acquisiton of low-cost housing
facilities by its members. This report praises the
combination of financial, social, and sanitation improvements achieved by the combined forces of CUNA,
the Peace Corps, the Food for Peace organization, and
UNICEF, all under AID leadership in the cooperative
work of numerous Latin American villages.

The testimony by CUNA's managing director, J.
Orrin Shipe, before Congressional committees in 1967
contains this credit-union success story:

> A local credit union in Ecuador hired a bus
> and arranged for a group of small farmers
> to take a trip to visit the nearest experi-
> mental farm. After seeing what could be
> accomplished, the farmers returned to their
> community and sought loans from the credit
> union for purposes such as hog production,
> chicken raising, and various other farming
> enterprises. The farmers thus combined
> capital with technical know-how. The in-
> creased earnings of the farmers resulted
> in an increase in savings, and the credit
> union then adopted a policy of planning its
> loan portfolio so that 80 per cent of the
> loans are made for agricultural production

purposes and the other 20 per cent for consumer or emergency purposes. . . . The
credit union was used as the basic vehicle
for helping to solve two of the developing
country's most pressing problems--housing
and agricultural production. When these
programs become more widespread in rural
areas, they may help to stem the migration
of people from rural to urban areas. In
the long run, the discouragement of migration will cost less than solving the problems
resulting from increased urbanization.

The chain-reaction effects of cooperative education and organization, combining credit and savings
policies after careful consideration of the individual conditions that prevail in a small region, can
hardly be overstated. One basic problem--which was
already solved before the CUNA activities began--is
how to find the right men for the preparatory work
in the region itself. They must be familiar with
and devoted to the cooperative idea, and have an ardent desire to help the people overcome their material
and spiritual poverty. A man with these qualifications is Father McLellan, who began in 1955, after
five years of preparatory efforts, to get twenty-three
Indians in Peru together for the establishment of a
credit cooperative. The society started with less
than $30 in deposits. It has grown into a 4,000-
member unit with $400,000 capital, and in ten years
was to spur the establishment of 200 similar cooperatives in Peru. Father McLellan's work has spread
over the whole of Peru with the help of $1 million
loan from the Inter-American Development Bank. The
200 societies are members of the Peru Credit Union
League, which belongs to the CUNA International organization. A Central Bank for Cooperatives has been
established in Peru and is the guarantor of the loan
mentioned above.

This extraordinary development has also been recognized in the May, 1962, issue of News for Farmer Cooperatives, published by the Farmer Cooperative Service,
U.S. Department of Agriculture. The publication emphasizes that one person's initiative led to the Peruvian
success--an accomplishment achieved in six years
under extremely difficult conditions. Although the

assistance lent to the movement by the CUNA organization soon after its first visible successes was great
help, this does not diminish Father McLellan's pioneer achievement. He was, as a Catholist priest,
particularly qualified for gaining the people's confidence in the face of the negative influence of the
radical political propaganda that then infiltrated
large parts of South America.

Religious leaders were of great help to the
CUNA movement in other regions also. A Jesuit priest,
who had observed cooperative enterprises in Honduras
and Samoa, initiated the same type of organizations
in the Fiji Islands. Beginning in 1954 with the establishment of sixty credit unions, a network of 250
units was eventually stretched over the islands. In
1960, after six years, there were more than 250,000
members and savings of nearly $2 million. Consider-
able help came from the British Governor of the
islands, who understood the value of the priest's undertaking. This help was more administrative than
financial. Government sources granted limited amounts
of credit for specific purposes only, such as the
supply of equipment and building material. The principle of self-support was thus preserved. In the absence of a law on cooperatives, the Governor issued
regulations for credit cooperatives and nominated a
registrar. From the very beginning, only natives
were recruited and employed in the cooperatives. On
the island of Veti Levu, one of the largest of the
Fiji group, savings were collected with the help of
a "bank on rails"--a specially equipped car that
visited every settlement to cash checks and, eventually, to disburse payments. A report issued by the
Governor of the Fiji Islands in 1960 emphasizes the
educational results of the credit-union movement,
mainly in the savings and financial habits of the
population, more than 50 per cent of which are Indian.

During his 1964 visit to the CUNA headquarters
in Madison, Wisconsin, the author received additional
evidence of the progress in the Fiji region. This
progress occurred where credit and savings cooperatives were built inside small communities or areas
by individuals who knew the people, their habits and

needs, and how to gain their confidence.

For those interested in a detailed drawing of all phases of establishing a credit-union project, the "Report on the Development of a Pilot Project in Directed Agricultural Production Credit through the 'Santa Teresita Limitada' Credit Union at Julio Andrade, Carchi - Ecuador" is highly recommended.* Copies may be obtained from CUNA International, Madison, Wisconsin.

CUNA support of all projects of this kind begins with an examination of the material and personal "feasibility" of a proposed establishment. If the conclusion is positive, the project is included in the common CUNA/AID Peace Corps program.

Then, in most cases, natives of the country are invited to participate in training courses in Madison and/or to get practical experience in working in an American cooperative. Peace Corps members chosen to go abroad are given parallel courses designed to prepare them for the special conditions that they will work under in building cooperatives in their assigned countries. Emphasis is given to the individual aspects involved in education for teamwork and in social consciousness. Next, credit-union techniques are taught. Special attention is paid to their characteristics as units based more on common personal (community and church) than on professional interests. In some circumstances, instruction is extended to cover other types of cooperatives in preparation for the role of credit unions in their development.

The methods, goals, and accomplishments of CUNA-type work in developing countries are in no way lessened by recognizing the system's limited applicability in some of the poorest regions. Where the cooperative movement is an integral part of a government's centrally administered policy, it is

---

*The report was prepared by Percy Avram, production credit specialist, AID/Ecuador/CUNA Program, and published in September, 1965, in Quito, Ecuador.

usually impossible to consolidate the over-all program of reforms and the political and social aspirations of the native leaders with the detailed work
required to build individually organized, small
groups of cooperators in locally restricted areas of
a country. This book would not do justice to its
main topic--sociological and psychological conditions under which cooperatives are built--if it neglected the social, political, and economic pressures
under which many governments have to act. These
pressures usually do not allow for the slow and
widely scattered beginnings of credit-union work.
The socioeconomic structure of the region and the
government's attitude toward progressive planning
determine the procedure to be used in building appropriate forms of cooperative establishments. The
existing programs become the framework for all subsequent undertakings and are often incompatible with
the individual work performed in small groups of
local unions.

This in no way excludes practicable ways of
combining the methods applied by CUNA with more comprehensive programs of organized credit. A government whose policy is not fixed by socialistic and
centralistic concepts may even welcome the idea of
an additional contribution, mainly through education
and internal organization, by way of the proved
credit-union method. Whether CUNA-like societies
can be built along with or in addition to other
already-existing credit and savings organizations depends on the specific circumstances in a region, as
well as the tact and skill used in approaching the
authorities.

The AID report to Congress of September, 1964,
calls the credit unions established with AID support
"the AID's most effective training institutions."
The agency's failure to mention other, more immediate
influences of credit-union work on a country's financial consolidation in general is a tacit recognition
of its limitations. Where swift and radical social
and economic moves are necessary to prevent the total
collapse of a nation's economy, as in some recently
emancipated African countries, or where, after the

overthrow of a reactionary administration, the revolutionary forces must take immediate steps to achieve
social progress, there is no alternative to a strongly centralized reorganization; decentralized undertakings are too slow. Remarkably, however, some
African governments have chosen, even under such
emergency conditions, to try cooperatives to provide
immediately required credit. Three examples were
given at the Cooperative Seminar for African Cooperators in Berlin, Summer, 1962:

After elimination of the colonial regime, the
Central African Republic was threatened with disaster
by the sudden interruption of coffee exports, the
country's main source of income. This interruption
was caused by the lack of facilities and the natives'
inability to prepare and process coffee of the quality demanded for export. The government established
ten financial institutions for granting loans to coffee cultivators and for continuing the operations of
processing plants. In order to overcome the distrust
of the coffee planters and ensure their participation
in the new institutions, the organizations were formally reorganized as cooperatives. Because of the
lack of appropriate preparations, all financial and
administrative functions were left to the government.
It succeeded in preventing a standstill in the export
trade, but failed with the new cooperatives. Nonetheless, the program remained in effect, and an institute for cooperative training in credit and other
monetary matters was established to prepare potential
members and officials for future self-administered
credit cooperatives.

Similar conditions endangered the economy of
the Ivory Coast after it achieved autonomy. Credit
was granted by the State Central Bank and distributed
through ad hoc regional offices called "cooperatives."
The positive reaction of parts of the population
made it possible for the government to replace most
of the material and personnel resources of the Europeans who had formerly handled all export operations
but had now left the country. Although the people's
assistance was confined to administrative work, it
was a useful way to give the people both confidence

and some basic knowledge of cooperative credit organizations. The Ivory Coast report evidenced the
government's recognition of the immediate necessity
to promote "the formation of independent capital with
savings" in order to reach genuine cooperative goals.

The Togo Government tried to solve its urgent
financial problems, which emerged after the etablish-
ment of self-administration, by reforming the former
Sociétés de Prévoyance under the new name of Sociétés
de Crédit Mutuel." About 500 were affiliated with
the State Bank, established in 1959. Because of the
recognized insufficiency of public funds, the Togo
representative acknowledged the preparatory status
of the above set-up, which was expected to form the
basis for private investments "to replace public
credit by saving."

The three African attempts to prevent an immediate breakdown of vital economic activities demonstrate the only way open to governments confronted
with such emergencies. They use their central power
to force upon the population provisional solutions
that, under normal circumstances, would hardly be acceptable. But even less acceptable would be criticism
by foreign advisers of such policies for not corresponding to "sound principles of cooperation."

Over the last few years, developing countries
have had many opportunities to exchange their views
and experiences involving monetary and credit policies, mainly in the agricultural sector, and to discuss their future financial plans. An outstanding
such meeting was the conference on the "Development
Center on Agricultural Credit for Africa" in Addis
Ababa, the capital of Ethiopia, sponsored by the FAO
and the African Economics Commission of the United
Nations. This was the FAO's fifth regional meeting
on agricultural credit. After the meetings in 1952
in Guatemala, in 1954 in Lebanon, in 1956 in Pakistan, and in 1958 in Brazil, the Addis Ababa meeting
in 1962 was organized for English-speaking Africans.
It was followed in 1965 by a meeting of representatives from French-speaking African countries.

The Addis Ababa meeting was attended by forty

representatives from seventeen countries, including
larger ones like Ethiopia, Ghana, Kenya, and Nigeria,
where agricultural credit is already partly organized
in cooperative form. Also attending were smaller
countries, like Basutoland, Njassa, Betshuana, and
Gambia, which had no cooperatives. The significance
attributed to cooperatively organized credit is expressed in the chapter "The Role of Cooperatives in
the Administration of Agricultural Credit," which
takes up twelve of the sixty pages of the official
conference report. The chapter on credit cooperatives
contains rather vague explanations and recommendations
for cooperative methods of building independent financial resources and savings. This vagueness results
from the disposition to compromise that is characteristic of a group of representatives of countries with
greatly differing cultural levels. The over-all picture of the discussions, as reflected in reports on
meetings of people in developing and more advanced
stages, is usually reduced to the lowest standard
represented at the meeting. In 1962, the more developed countries participating in the conference had
more than 7,000 cooperative societies with about 1
million members, paid-in capital and reserves of $33
million, and savings of $4 million. These amounts,
although low in comparison to the total agricultural-
credit requirements of these countries, are hopeful
beginnings of cooperative capital accumulations. The
conference agreed upon the importance of savings incentive and education, regardless of the mistrust
among the rural population, which was apparently the
major obstacle in all the countries represented.

The Addis Ababa report points to a particular
reason for building cooperatives that the author had
not observed elsewhere: Private banks in African
countries are said to grant short-term agricultural
credits as an advance against the expected harvest
income without securities on condition that any reliable organization relieve them of the burden of
collecting, storing, and selling the incoming products. Cooperative societies should be set up to take
over these functions. For this purpose, compulsory
crop deliveries should be imposed on members, and the
societies should dispose of appropriate warehouse
facilities. Cooperative action of this kind would

prevent governmental intrusion along with the inevitable controls. Corresponding government institutions
already exist in some African countries for the benefit of the above-mentioned system of private bank
credit. The conference members, however, felt that
cooperative regulations of a similar kind are prefer-
able, in as much as not all governments are in a position (or willing) to take over the job. Comparable
regulations exist for cocoa in Nigeria and for cotton
in Uganda, where delivery of the crop to government
marketing boards is compulsory. Authorized auction-
eers, occasionally employing licensed cooperative societies as purchasing agents, take care of realizing
the coffee crop in East Africa and tobacco in Rhodesia,
where the private banks accept the intermediary cooperatives as credit guarantors. The Addis Ababa conference report strongly recommends that cooperative
work be strengthened specifically where the security
problem for seasonal credits, from six to nine months,
is unsolved because of the lack of marketing boards
or similar agencies to administer the cooperatively
collected products. A plan was presented at the conference for the establishment of regional cooperative
banks with the government acting as guarantor for
private-bank credits; thus, local cooperative societies
would collect and sell the crop but would have the
help of authorized marketing institutions.

Although plans and proposals like those found in
the African report often show an astonishing degree
of inventiveness, they do not always truly benefit
credit policies. These plans reflect the contrast between declared goals and recognized obstacles to their
promotion; the former are based on the initial successes in already advancing countries, the latter reflect the lack of experience in the still less advanced countries, which have the same ambitions as
the former but don't know how to realize them.

A second chapter of the Addis Ababa report deals
with the middle- and long-term loans. In contrast
to the prospects for seasonal credits from private
banks, no such expectations were reported for longer
credit requirements. All kinds of guarantees for
creditors were discussed, without promising results,
including the different forms of joint cooperative

liability. Most of the conferees questioned the
value of cooperative liabilities, even in limited
form, as long as cooperative movements are in their
early stages.

In spite of the original conference decision
not to pass resolutions on credit policies and to
confine the meetings to an exchange of views and experiences, a twelve-point statement was finally
agreed upon and inserted in the report. This is a
substantial result of the Addis Ababa deliberations,
and some quotations are significant to include here:

"The best sources of credit for farmers are
cooperative societies or marketing boards, but other
arrangements may also be recommended in some regions."

"Training courses for individuals and employees
dealing with agricultural-credit matters in cooperative societies should be regularly introduced."

"The whole attitude of African farmers has to
be changed drastically if agricultural progress and
credit programs for farmers shall succeed. Such programs must be combined with technical training, marketing promotion, cooperative organization, and other
means of professional assistance."

These are the only three sentences in the concluding Addis Ababa statement that point to cooperatives in connection with improvement of agricultural-
credit systems. This is rather meager, in view of
cooperative performances in other developing countries and the participation of some experienced cooperators in the conference. It reflects the difficulty of reaching conclusions on existing conditions as well as future plans for larger regions.
Contacts between different developing countries are
increasingly useful; improvements in individual regions can be reported to other areas. But such ex-
changes of information are rarely of great value to
outsiders, who look for individual data on the already achieved and the still potential progress in
developing social and economic conditions in specific
regions.

The consensus expressed in combined reports by various neighboring countries generally regards equally obstructive symptoms only as bad climate, poor arability, feudal land tenure, settlement problems, lack of training, and illiteracy. These are too commonplace and hide the specific factors that vary from country to country, and sometimes even from district to district. The specific factors are the really relevant data on which to judge the applicability of both appropriate programs and the building of cooperatives as a highly individual means of social and economic progress. Thus, the minor emphasis on cooperative methods of credit supply should not discourage anybody who hopes to see cooperative developments in the countries represented at the conference table.

The diversity of conditions in neighboring countries was distinctly outlined in individual country reports presented at an International Training Center Seminar for leading cooperators in Madison, Wisconsin, held April to July, 1964. The following examples of cooperative credit work are quoted from a larger number of seminar contributions and indicate the impact of local conditions on financial and organizational progress. The essential conclusions of the reports to the Madison Center are shown by region:

AFRICA

Kenya, with a cooperative law in force since 1945, has about 600 cooperatives, most of them without capital formation of their own. Private banks are the main credit source. The administration promotes saving under a system of partial guarantees granted by the government. Some savings and loan associations came to life only in tribal settlements, where traditional ties and mutual confidence still prevail.

Uganda did not succeed in building up a notable cooperative movement, although legal regulations for cooperatives date from 1946. A small group of workmen's savings and loan associations are functioning, but they have not accumulated enough savings to cover the credit required by members. The rural population, half of which are tribesmen, belongs to a diversity of ethnic groups. As recently as Spring, 1966, Uganda (then called Buganda) was a combination of several more or less independent kingdoms. These present ethnic and recent historical facts explain the slow progress up to now, particularly regarding cooperative and other means toward organized credit.

Congo-Léopoldville was, for similar reasons of internal political unrest, in no position to overcome the rural population's aversion to cooperative-like methods that remind them of the hated Sociétés de Prévoyance of the Belgian administration. As early as 1956, a cooperative law was prepared, however, and efforts are being made to prepare the people for a new cooperative start.

Algeria, where the struggle for independence ended only recently, has made plans to convert certain vestiges of the French colonial administration into cooperative societies. The new government has retained the most unpopular methods used by the French--compulsory membership and taxlike contributions from the peasants, which are the only sources of agricultural credit until the planned credit and savings association can be established.

ASIA

Iraq, in contrast to most of its neighbors, began to activate its cooperative movement only during the second half of the 1950's, although a cooperative law has been in effect since 1944. The government is the main source of credit, and exercises tight controls on all credit applications. A Cooperative Central Bank, established in 1956, is exclusively financed by the government. It is to be completely transferred to the cooperative movement as soon as the latter's financial means are strong enough to provide for its capital and the credit required. The report gave no evidence of educational or other preparations for cooperative developments.

Jordan has more than 500 cooperative societies, half of which are rural credit cooperatives with unlimited liability. In addition, there are about 200 school cooperatives, which were established in connection with the government's extensive savings campaign. A State Institute for Cooperatives with a special Department for Credit and Saving surveys all activities connected with cooperative and other credit and savings matters. Government loans to cooperative societies are distributed by means of a Central Cooperative Society, whose capital shares are acquired by the cooperatives according to their credit requirements. The minimum number of shares purchasable is ten, two of which must be fully paid for before the membership rights--in essence the claim for and administration of credits--become valid. Urban credit cooperatives in Jordan made considerable progress and were, according to the report, able to finance with their own funds 60 per cent of the credits granted to members. These urban savings and loan associations are usually formed by salaried employees. The credit-cooperative movement in Jordan is extended to self-help insurance protection against sickness, unemployment, disability, and old age. In 1962, most credit cooperatives began to provide insurance for outstanding loans by charging a premium of 3/4 per cent on the open balances.

Nepal's cooperative movement is exclusively governed and financed by the state. Between 1957 and 1963, 900 cooperative societies were established, 200 of them credit cooperatives.

Thailand is one of the most active countries in promoting savings. Ten thousand village cooperatives and more than 100 urban savings and loan associations were in operation in 1962. The government promotes cooperatives with the help of its College for Economic and Cooperative Science. "Cooperation" is a compulsory subject in the curricula of all elementary and high schools.

LATIN AMERICA

Colombia is one of the Middle and South American

countries where the CUNA influence is the dominating
factor in cooperative progress. From 1961 through
1964, CUNA activities have helped to increase the
number of credit unions in the country from 50 to
more than 300.

Trinidad: The credit cooperative movement began slowly in 1939. The small island had 320 credit
unions and 140 school cooperatives in 1964. A cooperative central bank, established in 1956, is fully
financed by credit-union funds. The government makes
no contributions other than for salaries of central-
bank officials.

The report was presented by the founder and
leader of a larger savings and credit cooperative in
Trinidad. His union has about 100 members who have
contributed the equivalent of $25,000 to the coopera-
tive funds. Credits are normally granted for three
years, but usually amortized in shorter terms. Of
148 loans granted in 1963, totaling $18,000, nearly
$15,000 were repaid before the end of 1964. He stated
that the data on his society are typical of the accomplishments of most of the country's credit unions.

The above-quoted ten reports, presented in 1964
to the International Cooperative Training Center in
Madison, clearly prove that regional or other global
accounts of the conditions and developments in larger areas can never provide the information required
to recognize the main factors that characterize the
status and the trends pertaining to individual areas.
Neither the region to which a country belongs, nor
its size, nor any other general criterion determines
the progress of its cooperative institutions, particularly with regard to those having credit and savings as their backbone.

From each country's individual condition, as
reviewed above, there are four main groups into which
the ten countries may be divided: a) countries still
hampered by the consequences of recent wars and/or
revolutions that impose the deferment of all plans
or existing programs to build cooperative establishments (for example, Algeria, Congo, Uganda);

b) countries with no cooperative initiative other
than by governmental action (for example, Iraq,
Nepal, Kenya); c) countries where old traditions of
similar character have been mobilized and successfully applied to modern methods of cooperation (for
example, Thailand), or where the government has succeeded in reanimating (and adapting to internal requirements) cooperative institutions established
under a colonial regime and since then more or less
forgotten (Jordan); d) countries where missionary
initiative combined with foreign assistance built
cooperative movements (Colombia and Trinidad). These
were based on careful detail work with individual
groups of natives, and were backed by international
agencies such as the Pan American Union, the Alliance
for Progress, CUNA, and AID.

Jordan, grouped above under (c), may also be
regarded in the light of regional influences, and so
represent an exceptional case of adaptation to neighboring conditions. The government's success in re-
building the inactive cooperatives of the past cannot
be explained without reference to outside stimula-
tion, since feudal and other reactionary forces within the country are still strong. Such stimulus may
have come from neighboring Israel, with its widespread
cooperative organization and experiences. Several
developing countries have asked for help and advice
from Israeli experts in building up their own cooperatives. Although similar arrangements between
Jordan and Israel were politically unthinkable, some
unofficial means of communication between immediate
neighbors is always open. This is particularly true
where people's attention is caught by such contrasting situations as the social progress in Israel and,
until recently, the stagnation in Jordan. Whether
or not a Jordan/Israel case of regional intercourse
in matters such as cooperatives can be admitted, the
overriding importance of internal factors in the application of socioeconomic reforms--for example,
credit and savings inducements in areas with primitive populations--cannot be challenged.

The FAO has published a <u>Guide to Methods and</u>

Procedures of Rural Credit Surveys (Rome, Italy,
1962), written by the FAO adviser T. S. Rao of the
Department of Agricultural Credit of the Indian Reserve Bank. Although not particularly directed toward cooperative credit institutions, the Guide contains valuable information for cooperatives in its
complex survey of all methods of credit distribution,
particularly regarding the problem of coordinating
credit policies with the general goals of economic-
development programs.

A much broader investigation was launched by
the FAO, in consultation with the ICA, covering all
aspects of "Financing Agricultural Development
Through Cooperatives and Other Institutions." A
group of experts from various countries (Sweden,
Holland, Germany, Italy, India, and Paraguay) divided into two subgroups, alternately visiting Ceylon, Iraq, the Ivory Coast, Libya, Malaya, Somalia,
and Tanganyika over a period of three months. A
condensed report of their findings was published,
and the results are particularly interesting, especially some basic observations by these experts and
their urgent demand for an improvement in the efficiency of credit-cooperative work:

Utilization of Credit:

> The development of agriculture in most
> countries has not yet reached the stage
> that the average medium size and small
> farmer makes an appropriate use of the
> credit facilities extended to him. This
> phenomenon is due to an obvious lack of
> knowledge as to how to use credit in the
> most profitable manner as well as the con-
> ditions inherent to the prevailing socio-
> economic pattern of rural life and to the
> farmer's traditional approach to problems
> of agricultural production. It proved
> not always to be sufficiently realized
> that in the initial stages of agricultural
> development, finance to farmers must have
> a predominantly consumptive character.
> As long as agriculture is not a business

but a way of life, cost price a sheer fic-
tion, and farm and household expenditure an
inextricable knot, it will be impossible to
make a clear distinction between credit for
productive and for consumptive purposes.

Agricultural Credit Institutions in General:

It was found that the approach of many
credit institutions to the problem of agricultural credit was passive and traditional . . .   Instead of considering repayment
capacity as the sheet anchor of all agricultural credit, incommensurate importance
was often attached to the security of real
estate . . . Apprehension of taking risks
and of incurring high expenditure incited
them too often to extending credit to the
bigger farmers only and to neglecting the
small agriculturist. Complaints were often
heard regarding cumbersome loan procedures,
too low credit limits and too late disburse-
ment of loans . . . In most countries the
moneylender-trade-shopkeeper is still the
most important source of rural credit . . .
It was also noticed that services in the
field of supply and marketing rendered to
small farmers by non-cooperative credit institutions or cooperative societies were very
inadequate. It was often insufficiently realized that credit can only have a sufficient
impact if supply, storage, marketing and
sometimes processing are properly organized.

Cooperative Credit Institutions:

Though the situation proved to be different from country to country and even from
district to district, it was found that particularly in the less advanced areas the
prerequisites for the existence of strong,
active and efficient autonomous cooperative
societies at the primary level were usually
not or insufficiently filled. Autoactivity,
autonomie and autofinance in cooperative
societies were generally speaking very weak.

Except in some rare cases, savings were insignificant. The interest taken by the average farmer in the cooperative movement left much to be desired and was often completely absent. For these reasons government guidance, supervision, technical assistance and finance will be for a long time indispensable, if cooperation is to become an efficient instrument for agricultural development. The name "cooperation" was found to cover a variety of organizations ranging from almost fully government controlled, guided, supervised and financed institutions with compulsory membership to cooperative societies organized more or less on the classical lines but subject to a fair amount of government interference. . . .

On several occasions it was stated that cooperatives were misused for political purposes which in some cases lead to their being discredited in the eyes of the farmers. . . .

<u>Since all shortcomings mentioned in this section are not inherent to the cooperative system as such, the Group is convinced that cooperative societies are the most suited instrument for bringing about rural development.</u>[8]   (Author's emphasis.)

The judgment expressed in the last paragraph, after so many critical remarks, summarizes the observations made in an extensive study of eight geographically different regions. This conclusion should give additional impetus to all those interested in building cooperative movements in developing countries.

Not immediately connected with cooperative methods of financing, but of no less importance to their application, is a finding in Part III of the report entitled "Some of the Group's Main Conclusions and Recommendations." The subparagraph of this part, dealing with international finance, contains the following statements:

The Group is of the opinion that, if the
central banks of all developing countries
were sufficiently agricultural-credit-minded
and took adequate measures to finance properly agricultural credit institutions, the over-
whelming part of the funds needed to finance
agricultural credit to farmers and their organizations could be provided by them without
any dangerous inflationary effect. . . .

Rather than the expansion of the volume
of credit, the main problem in most countries
is that the existing credit organizations are
inadequately organized to be able to absorb
properly the volume of finance available and
to ensure that the growth of agricultural
credit is not faster than the growth of agricultural production, in other words, that
they are unable to see that a proper use is
made of the loans they provide. . . .

The Group fears that the idea, as though
sheer pumping in substantial funds derived
from international sources would be able to
make a major contribution to strengthening the
agricultural structure, is an illusion and
might even prove to be a fallacy. The Group
is convinced that the chief driving power in
the matter of financing credit to farmers
and their organizations should and could come
from the developing countries themselves.[9]

Recommendations follow on improving the organization of credit institutions of all types and on
modernizing and intensifying the modes of training
credit personnel on all levels. International funds
are recommended for these purposes, rather than for
immediate credits to agricultural loan distributors
in the developing countries.

The foregoing conclusions and recommendations
call for further efforts to intensify cooperative
saving and credit policies. In the experts' view,
the developing countries' own financial means are
adequate to make sufficient loans available for extending and improving their agricultural economy

"without any dangerous inflationary effect." This
view presupposes that the cooperative organizations
succeed in refunding the capital and loan funds initially provided by their governments, i.e., in accumulating enough savings to stand on their own feet,
at least temporarily, and so to enable their governments to use the available money as revolving funds
to finance agricultural credit requirements.

This seems to the author to be the main lesson to be drawn from the conclusions reached by the
group of experts. Their investigations and resulting
statements belong to the most extended and authoritative deeds of this kind recently performed in the
field of agricultural credit.

It remains to be seen, if, how, and when public
and private organizations of countries helping develop agricultural progress in poor regions act
to reduce the volume of credit hitherto granted for
this purpose. The eventual consequences will be felt
primarily by the developing countries' lending financial bodies. Immediate adaptation is beyond the ca-
pability, however, of cooperative movements. All
they can do is to prepare all human and material
forces at their disposal for as much financial independence as possible, i.e., to accelerate their efforts, which in any event are required to reach this
genuinely cooperative goal.

COOPERATIVE INSURANCE

Insurance in general is a particular form of
saving, especially in the initial stages of application.

The report on cooperatives in Jordan, referred
to earlier, is the only documentation of cooperative
insurance establishments to be found in the immediate
reports from developing countries used in this book.
At the time of his visit to CUNA headquarters in Madison, the author obtained evidence of the Latin
American Credit Union League's adherence to the CUNA
insurance system, which is concentrated in the

CUNA-Mutual Insurance Company.

Two major types of insurance are involved. They are both obligatory in the United States and Canadian credit-union movements in general: 1) loan insurance covering debts that are due when the debtor dies (premium 1/3 of 1 per cent per annum in addition to regular interest); 2) life insurance connected with savings in the amount of twice the balance of the savings account at death--three times if the death is caused by an accident--(premium 3/4 of 1 per cent per annum). Both these types of insurance protect the debit or credit balances during the lifetime of the debtors or creditors and so are highly recommended for countries where a lack of confidence hampers credit and savings developments. This, of course, conditions insurance facilities that, for the time being, do not exist, and can hardly be expected to be established in most developing countries, particularly where governments control the cooperative movement. No doubt exists, however, that all kinds of cooperatively self-administered insurance institutions will be of great help, and even urgently required, in later stages of cooperative developments.

In view of this factor, in 1960, the International Cooperative Alliance appointed a committee to prepare a report--for presentation to the Alliance's International Conference in 1963--on the results of a comprehensive study of the possibilities for introducing cooperative insurance facilities into developing countries. The committee Research Report, issued in 1962, reviewed existing insurance institutions in some developing countries and the steps taken by some cooperative organizations in Western countries to prepare corresponding establishments, mainly for training purposes. The report noted that three larger cooperative insurance societies existed in the regions under review, and all three were in India. The three were:

1) The Cooperative General Insurance Society in Hyderabad, established in 1947 by cooperatives in the State of Hyderabad, began operating in 1949. It covered fire and transportation damages throughout India,

but not life insurance, which was a state monopoly.
The Society's capital shares are mainly owned by
cooperatives. The governmental registrar of cooperatives is an ex officio member of the Society's Board
of Directors.

2) The Union Cooperative Insurance Society in
Bombay. Registered in 1949, the society began to
operate in 1951. Its structure and activities resemble those of the Hyderabad Society.

3) The Malaya Cooperative Insurance Society in
Kuala Lumpur, Malaya, was established in 1954 and
began operating in 1956. The Society handled life
insurance exclusively, but planned to add fire insurance later. It covered the whole of Malaya and
Singapore. The report contains no data on the three
societies' business volume or the first periods of
activity.

The committee recommends setting up no new cooperative insurance establishments unless feasibility
studies have proved that the means and conditions in
a region justify such plans.

The following preparatory work was in progress
at the time of the committee's investigations:

A training center for young cooperators from
developing countries has been established by the
Swiss Re-insurance Company in Zurich. Courses in
English and German are open to carefully chosen, already prepared trainees, with no more than twelve
men per course. French and Spanish courses will be
added to the program, which covers all branches of
the insurance business.

In 1960, six leaders of different branches of
the Swedish Cooperative Insurance Organization visited Pakistan, India, Thailand, Burma, and Malaya,
studying these countries' needs and conditions regarding insurance cooperatives. Another study was
made a year later in Greece, Turkey, Syria, Egypt,
and Jordan. Similar visits to African countries were
scheduled. The Swedish Organization planned to

establish a Southeast Asian Seminar for Cooperative
Insurance in New Delhi as a first practical measure.

The Cooperative Insurance Company of England
has also been active in conducting training for cooperative insurance work in some countries abroad.
A number of Ghanaians were trained in preparation for
the then planned establishment of a National Cooperative Insurance Company of Ghana. The British organization also opened its courses to interested cooperators from Turkey and Malaya. But, up to the time
of the report, only the Ghana project had led to
positive steps for an insurance cooperative.

The Committee Report of the International Cooperative Alliance clearly indicates a reserved attitude toward early promotion of insurance cooperatives
in developing countries. It repeatedly stresses the
necessity to carefully study the needs of both a
country and its population before undertaking concrete
proposals for insurance cooperatives. The committee's
conclusions are basically the same as those expressed
in this book, and emphasize the sociological and psychological aspects of establishing cooperative institutions in developing countries.

NOTES TO CHAPTER 4

1. German Central Bank for Cooperatives, data
issued as "Foreign Trade Information," June, 1967.

2. Martin A. Abrahamsen, <u>A Look at Agricultural
Cooperatives in India</u> (Washington, D.C.: Farmer
Cooperative Service, U.S. Department of Agriculture,
1961).

3. U.S. Department of Agriculture, <u>News for
Farmer Cooperatives</u> (the official organ of the
Farmer Cooperative Service) (April, 1962).

4. <u>1960 Report to the German Cooperative Seminar for Developing Countries.</u>

5. See <u>Credit Union Magazine</u> (October, 1964 – March, 1965).

6. <u>Ibid.</u> (July, 1967), pp. 40 ff.

7. See the Agency for International Development reports to Congress on help to cooperatives in developing countries (2nd and 3rd reports; Washington, D.C., 1963 and 1964).

8. FAO, <u>Land Reform</u> (July, 1964), pp. 34–46.

9. <u>Ibid</u>.

CHAPTER **5** WAYS AND MEANS OF
COOPERATIVE EDUCATION

Education is a constant factor in cooperative
work. Even in countries with old traditions and
well-established cooperative organizations, it is
the backbone of every new attempt to create such
movements. The object of the present chapter is not
to demonstrate the need but rather to illustrate the
many-sided ways and means of introducing such education in various developing countries.

The literature on education and training in cooperatives has grown so much in recent years that
some organizations have issued bibliographical lists
of such publications, with periodical supplements.
Some examples of this material, which altogether comprises several hundred pages, are included in the
bibliography to this volume. The following presentation does not attempt to compete with this abun-
dance; rather, it seeks to evaluate the educational
methods and institutions observed by the author, together with those reported from other sources. The
author has discussed most of them with competent
people in developing, as well as in Western, countries. This exchange of experiences and ideas is
reflected in the following records and statements.

It follows from earlier considerations of the
government's role in building cooperative movements
that education is a difficult problem where close
ties connect the state and the cooperatives. This
is particularly true of nominal cooperatives, hastily
set up by the government merely to serve its
politico-economic (or merely political) goals. This
action shows the government's disregard for the es-
sentials of cooperative principles. Even where

former cooperative practices or similar traditions among the population have been restored, the deviation from genuine cooperative motivations is incompatible with the principle of autonomy as a primary objective of cooperative education.

The mere existence, however, of an association of men in a cooperative justifies expectations of gradually rising educational opportunities and effects. Examples are numerous. Landless rural workers, nomads, and others have been settled in cooperative units by the Egyptian, the Iranian, and other governments for the purpose of land reform, amelioration, and similar programs. Initially totally unqualified for group action, they were integrated into organized units and first discovered how to act jointly and to learn the requirements and advantages of group work. This was the first result of merely practical and technical directions. As time went on, they began to understand the functions and underlying ideas of cooperation, a long but promising undertaking. A prerequisite for this is the state's interest in selecting as leaders of the quasi cooperatives only men who know or can learn to combine technical and socio-ideological instruction and who favor genuine cooperatives in their country. But often there are merely political reasons for establishing cooperatives in developing countries, and sometimes inexperience is an obstacle to self-administration and educational programs. It is a challenge for Western advisers on cooperatives to try, under these circumstances, to persuade authorities of the need for education. As previously noted, this kind of advice must be given tactfully and cautiously in order to avoid creating resentment. Where political prejudice exists, it can be overcome by this approach. In general, it is easier to win the support of officials of groups of cooperatively organized people than to overcome the opposition of men in the higher ranks of government who have had neither geographical nor ideological contact with functioning cooperatives.

Lack of personal contact often aggravates preconceptions such as the frequently heard idea that

social and spiritual directives are premature in the
early stages of development. This objection is, in
most cases, merely a pretext; the real fear is of
the political consequences of liberal education.

One of the most effective training schools for
young cooperative officials and members, which the
author inspected, was in Alexandria, Egypt. Established in 1952 and enlarged in 1960, it is administered by a Board of Directors representing the Central Organizations of Egypt's different cooperative
branches, the Agricultural Credit Bank of Egypt, and
the competent governmental departments. Three categories of teachers are employed: 1) retired officials of cooperative administrations, 2) active cooperators in leading positions, and 3) members of
university faculties with curricula in cooperative
matters. This combination brings together old and
new skills, practical and theoretical knowledge. The
courses are relatively short, in spite of their complex programs. Passing the final examination is a
prerequisite for advancement in any Egyptian cooperative.

Cooperative courses are also taught by the Department of Agriculture and the Department of Commerce at the El-Shams University in Cairo. Usually
these courses are taken as a minor subject, and the
students are not expected to become either professional cooperators or officials. The curricula of
both departments are remarkably comprehensive. The
shortage of cooperative teachers became a real problem when, early in 1962, the Central Organization
of Agricultural Cooperatives announced the immediate
establishment of 124 cooperative training centers in
all districts of the country. Elaborate programs
for members, employees, supervisors, and others were
set up in order to overcome the lack of efficient
cooperative management and reliable control. But no
instructors for the 124 centers were available. The
author was informed by the chief of the office in
charge of organizing the training centers that some
100 university students would be employed, most of
them still in the initial stages of their studies,
and all without cooperative practice and lecture

experience. Accelerated special courses would prepare them for filling the vacancies in time. In
response to the author's question of why the public
announcement had not been postponed until enough instructors were trained, the official declared that
the centers would only become viable under immediate
pressure. If only ten or twenty centers became active over several months, this would be enough to
get the program going. Otherwise, it would never
become active. This is typical of the radical methods
often applied in developing countries and of the optimism about the efficacy of drastic action. This
is not criticism. Radicalism and optimism are among
the psychological factors that are characteristic
of leadership in developing countries. The ensuing
spontaneity may often lead to wrong decisions, but
it is a fortunate talent among men who are striving
for progress and have neither the information nor
the time required to determine the feasibility of
each project. Education, especially, can be inspired by such leaders. These men are less reluctant
than others to compel the use of educational programs
proposed by foreign advisers, which may bring about
radical reforms and depend for their implementation
on the courage and energy of competent leaders.

The foregoing remarks on cooperative training
institutions in Egypt have to be supplemented by
reference to the educational work performed by foreigners. Some international agencies contribute to
cooperative education in many developing countries.
Their activities in Egypt were usually independent
from the government's own training programs. In
discussions of this, some officials in the respective
administrations repeatedly pointed to the absence of
coordination between the two groups. Although conflicting interests may sometimes arise, these may be
outweighed by the advantages of the extended educational facilities and aspects offered by various international organizations to the Egyptian cooperative
movement.

The FAO's Central Office for the Near East is
in Cairo. Its chief officer was, at the time of the
author's visit, Dr. A. R. Sidky, the former Minister

of Agriculture and one of the organizers of Egypt's
new agricultural cooperative movement. His experience and keen interest in education provides the competent authorities with all the resources that the
FAO makes available. He expressed the view that the
educational needs in his country's agricultural sector require a "more organic" (less uniform) formation
of the cooperative institutions. He had been working
toward this end by steadily strengthening the ties
between the FAO and Egypt's cooperatives.

Four times between 1957 and 1961, groups of ILO
experts were assigned to study the cooperative organizations in Egypt, paying specific attention to training activities. Some of the courses established in
Alexandria and Cairo, the author was told, were based
on recommendations made by ILO experts.

Additional educational assistance was provided
by UNESCO, which is one of the founders of the Arab
States Training Center for Education for Community
Developments (ASFEC) near Cairo. The center was organized in 1952 in compliance with an agreement
reached between the Government of Egypt and the found-
ing institutions UNESCO, FAO, WHO, and ILO. At the
Center, social workers of different Arab states are
trained in all branches of rural community life. The
courses last from two to six months, and include cooperation and methods of cooperative education. After
an extended visit to the Center's large and well-
equipped installations, where a representative of the
Ministry of Education, assisted by two Arab members
of UNESCO, explained and demonstrated the work being
performed, the author was invited to visit a nearby
village, one of the places where Center trainees
carry out practical social work during the last weeks
of their courses. Two young trainees--an Egyptian
and a Sudanese--assigned to the village, together
with the leader of the local cooperative, showed the
author everything connected with the community's social development. Their enthusiasm and the apparent
agreement between them and the cooperative manager
were impressive indications of the Center's successful operations. The village offered a remarkable
example of the coordination and integration of

cooperative and other social activities in a rural
community.

Educational tendencies and institutions in various developing countries were interpreted by participants in the International Cooperative Seminars of
the German Foundation for Developing Countries in
Berlin in 1960 and 1962. The following extracts
from their reports reflect the great variety of regional and sociological factors and conditions that
affect the approach to and the results of cooperative
education.

Iran. Selected graduates of Iran's agricultural
schools are prepared for cooperative work in three
training courses in universities, agricultural banks,
and training centers. Financial training is emphasized at the Institute for Cooperative Credit and
the Cooperative Seminar, both attached to the Bank
of Agriculture.

However, the country's leading financial institution, the State Bank of Iran, expressed disapproval
of this curriculum. One of its most recent annual
reports stated that banking and related matters are
only one component of cooperative work, and the
trainees should, for the most part, be prepared by
practical work in cooperatives. This practical education should be deepened, later on, by studies in
cooperatives in progressive countries.

India. The conflict between centralization and
decentralization that characterizes the different
trends in India's cooperative movement was also expressed in the attitudes toward education found in
the two separate reports presented to one of the
seminars. The first Indian delegate asked separate
education for leaders and members of cooperatives
and for government officials and supervisory personnel. Education of the first group, he said,
should be left to regional and local agencies of the
All India Cooperative Union, the country's leading
cooperative organization. The second category should
be trained by branches of the Central Committee for
Cooperative Education, a government institution

controlled by the state and the Reserve Bank of
India.

The report of the other Indian representative,
a government-trained registrar, omitted any mention
of education outside public institutions. Without
the preceding report, the seminar would have been
under the impression that no independent resources
exist in India to prepare cooperators for work in
regions with the most divergent customs and traditions. Although the registrar emphasized a program
of education for self-administration, he based it
exclusively on his concept of centralization--uniform
curricula compiled and controlled by the Central Committee for Cooperative Education.

West Pakistan. Educational matters were touched
on in the report only in reference to building the
staffs of agricultural and cooperative instructors in
governmental agencies. Nothing was said about cooperative education. However, the remarkable principle
was stated that the instructors must be trained to
be "friends and teachers" of the rural population in
order to develop "cooperative leaders with a sense
of responsibility" instead of merely "talking the
peasants into cooperation."

Niger. The government did not believe that cooperative education could be carried out without
first training its nationals for this purpose in foreign countries. Selected trainees were to be assigned
to study at the Center National de la Coopération
Agricole in Paris. The Nigerian report claimed that,
after the techniques of cooperative education, the
students were supposed to learn how to "educate for
honesty" and how to "develop mutual confidence" before qualifying as educators in Niger.

Cameroun. As in Niger, the government left the
preparation of cooperative instructors to the Center
in Paris. Beginning in 1952, two or three selected
students were designated every year for the French
Center's training courses.

Central African Republic. A special government

agency organizes training courses in various regions
of the country. The basic ideas of cooperation are
outlined and recommended to the general population
through regular radio broadcasts.

Of course, reports like the foregoing never provide enough insight into the actual developments in
the educational field to allow any judgment on the
methods applied. Even though most of the countries
appeared to be still in the earliest stages of planning at the time of these reports, it is encouraging
to realize the concern of most governments for the
educational aspects of cooperation. This is primarily true of the African areas. Two of the three reports from African countries revealed that the government had no educational programs and relied exclusively on foreign assistance. The reports from
the Asian countries--India, Iran, West Pakistan--
reflect more advanced stages of education in which
different methods are used and conflicting ideas of
cooperative education compete with each other. However, these first signs of self-determination do not
exclude the need of foreign advice and assistance,
which are equally required in countries where well-
established educational systems have been altered or
destroyed by violent political or social disturbances.

A drastic example of retrogression caused by
several decades of war and internal disturbances was
the educational system of the Greek cooperative movement. The State Cooperative School was closed in
1937, the school operated by the movement's central
organization closed in 1946, and meanwhile cooperative education was eliminated from the curricula of
universities and vocational schools. During the
1950's, the cooperative movement of Greece slowly
began to rebuild its organization, and around 1960
the Panhellenic Confederation of Unions of Agricultural Cooperatives initiated new educational institutions. When the Confederation asked the German
Raiffeisen Association (Central Organization of the
German Rural Cooperatives) for advice, Dr. Waidelich
went to Greece and helped the Confederation establish
a new educational program. Dr. Waidelich recommended, among other improvements, a decentralized system

of training courses to replace the seminar in Athens and the assignment of young cooperators to schools and practical work in German cooperatives.

The disrupting impact of wars and revolutions on cooperative education is an extreme manifestation of the damage that cooperatives always suffer if they engage in politics. The Greeks are a politically oriented people, and so the purging of the cooperative movement of partisan influences, which lasted for many years after the main internal struggles were over, may have been more difficult in Greece than in other countries. In principle, however, wherever governments use cooperatives to achieve their specific ends, the disturbing influence of politics on cooperative education is the same as long as political unrest prevails. It is for this reason that the neutralizing effect of American and European assistance to educational programs and institutions is so urgently required. It is often the only medium to counterbalance one-sided political trends.

This particular point of view has repeatedly been discussed by American cooperative leaders and the author. Foreign advisers sometimes insist so strongly on educational reforms that they hold that all assistance should cease whenever their educational recommendations are not accepted.

In connections with this discussion, a representative of the Cooperative League of America granted the author permission to use the following two reports by leaders of cooperative schools in Vietnam and Nyasaland (Malawi). These schools are sponsored by the League and were established by its agents. The Vietnam report covers 1959-61, the Nyasaland report 1962-64. Both reports show the potentialities of individually oriented means of cooperative education when unhampered by political interference.

Vietnam. After enactment of a cooperative law in 1954 and establishment of an agricultural central credit institute in 1957, the government asked for advice about cooperative education from American organizations. The following Principles and Goals were among those agreed upon, and they form the program of the Cooperative Training Center, established with American help immediately thereafter and opened in 1959: "The cooperative movement belongs to the people." "Training and education have to be extended to all levels of the movement." "Member education shall be performed in small groups." "Cooperative education is likewise required for peasants, fishermen, and craftsmen." "The mental education of the individuals involved is more important than the technical training."

Four types of course were inaugurated:

1) Basic training for cooperative officials (from four to twelve months).

2) Refresher courses for cooperative officials after a specified period of employment (from two weeks to two months).

3) Seminars for officials who are outside the cooperatives but whose assignments are connected with cooperative work (from three to six days).

4) Membership training courses (from two to three weeks).

The most extensive--a full year's basic training--comprised more than 900 lectures (three per day). About 500 dealt with administration and organization, about 300 with cooperative economics and the law, and about 100 with social matters.

After an initial participation of 429 persons in 1959, the courses were attended by 1,092 in 1960, and by 2,438 in 1962. Basic education of members and employees was undertaken, as well as local courses all over the country in cooperatives and other peasant organizations. Nearly 12,000 people participated in the first three years.

A game method of instruction was developed in the center's courses and has proved to be very effective in introducing members of different professions

who lacked knowledge of cooperative ideas and methods
into this new way of personal and professional behavior. Each participant is assigned an individual
role according to his normal life and environment.
The teacher leads the group in playing their roles
as students and teachers and acting out what is involved in joining a cooperative, what its functions
and regulations are, how to use its facilities, and
how to behave at membership meetings. A textbook
has been issued for teachers on how to introduce and
practice the game method and is one of their most
important educational tools.

The cooperative societies were invited by the
Center to report on their experiences with officials
and members trained in some of the courses and to
offer critical comments and suggestions for improvements to the Center's administration.

The head of the Vietnam Center, C. H. Hutchinson, adds to his report above some recommendations
of particular relevance to foreign advisers and those
engaged in cooperative educational work in developing countries:

1) New concepts and skills will be understood
by native populations only if they are taught and
explained in terms derived from the people's traditional working habits, values, and inherited ideas.

2) Native officials must be persuaded that the
new working habits that they are supposed to learn
as well as to communicate are appropriate for attaining progress under their country's specific conditions
and that they are not mere foreign copies and that
they are not imposed by force.

3) Foreign advisers should constantly work toward increasing the native leaders' independence
from foreign aid.

In support of his recommendations, Mr. Hutchinson refers to his observations of how the Vietnamese
are striving for a free life, autonomy, and self-
determination, and concludes that the cooperative

movement and the educational preparation for it, as
carried out in the Training Center, are of great
significance to large parts of the Vietnamese population.

Since the above paragraphs were written, several
years of war and internal unrest have plagued Vietnam, and destroyed much of what had been built. Mr.
Hutchinson's remarks demonstrate the soundness of
the fight for liberty that is now going on in Vietnam.

The second report on educational assistance
given in recent years by the Cooperative League of
America was presented by Lyle Anderson, a League representative who went to Nyasaland at that government's request for advice and assistance in cooperative education. Mr. Anderson stayed in Nyasaland
from 1962 to 1964, and issued his report shortly
after his return to the United States in March, 1964.

While Nyasaland was under a British protectorate,
a cooperative law was enacted in 1947, and a Cooperative Department was established in one of the
government's departments. Cooperative societies for
producing and marketing purposes were organized, administered, and financed mainly by the government.
Their initial successes, however, did not survive
the period of internal struggles (1953-61) prior to
independence. The new Prime Minister, Dr. H. K. Banda,
began to reorganize the cooperative movement immediately after political stabilization was achieved,
and inaugurated the first cooperative school in
October, 1962. The school was run by Mr. Anderson.
He had the help of two native leaders, who had been
trained in the United States to be cooperative teachers.

Dr. Banda in his inauguration address declared:

1) Cooperatives based on the initiative of the
government are to be rejected. The formation of
self-financed societies must be the goal of cooperative developments.

2) The government cannot be expected to grant

any financial assistance, before cooperative members
have made investments on their own.

3) As soon as possible, self-administration by
the societies' own members has to be established.

Mr. Anderson and his assistants toured large
parts of the country before making detailed plans
for the first courses and a general program. They
lectured, mainly where the government's previously
established Farm Marketing Boards were located, and
they participated in the Credit Union Conference in
Dar-es-Salaam, Tanganyika, sponsored by CUNA for
representatives of the credit-union movements from
Rhodesia, Uganda, Kenya, Zanzibar, Tanganyika, and
Nyasaland. This visit contributed to a coordination
of cooperative-educational programs in the neighboring countries.

After the tour, a program for the school was
presented to the Ministry of Commerce and, on its
recommendation, approved by the Prime Minister in
1963. It was built around practical instruction,
carefully adapted to the particular interests of individual groups of the population. Initially, most
participants were interested in credit-union work,
and all phases of its operation were practiced by
organizing the pupils into a credit union. Courses
lasted for more than six months. Other courses were
established for educators in rural communities, for
members and employees, and for officials experienced
in public administration.

An appendix to Mr. Anderson's report shows a
statement presented to him, as leader of the school,
by a group of those who participated in the first
course. It sets forth the objectives of cooperative
education that these men thought were most important
to their country. They felt that trainees should be
taught to pay close attention to the productive potentialities of their homeland; they should learn
to respect rural, as well as industrial, labor; they
should understand what initiative and responsibility
really mean and can achieve; and they must be taught
to forgo luxury and to recognize the value of saving.

In addition, they believed that the school should
help to create an equal chance at education for
everybody, and the knowledge of what cooperation can
contribute to this end.

The students' postulates clearly demonstrate
that they have learned some of the fundamentals of
cooperative means and goals.

Mr. Anderson's report contains two letters from
students that he received after his return to the
United States. They express deep appreciation of
the principles and methods applied in the school,
and testify to the specific usefulness of independent
and individually oriented ways of education, based
on careful preparation and adapted to the ever-
changing conditions under which formerly oppressed
populations try to meet the requirements of modern
society.

In addition to the reports of the Cooperative
League cited above, other reports are quoted in the
following paragraphs to demonstrate the great variety
of educational developments, under divergent conditions, that predetermine the methods to be applied:

Nigeria. In contrast to its northern neighbor,
the Republic of Niger (a very poor country that only
recently made plans to develop a cooperative movement), the Republic of Nigeria, formerly under a
British protectorate, is well acquainted with different types of cooperative societies and has three
cooperative schools, organized after British models.
Dr. Waidelich visited Nigeria and reported in April,
1963, that the cooperative schools in Nigeria offered
a "fully developed educational system." They are
financed by the government, which, after independence,
did not allow an interruption in the functioning of
the cooperative institutions created by the former
British administration. It employed economists and
teachers who were trained in England as cooperative
educators. Courses for officials and supervisors
take nine months, plus one month of practical work,
and form the basis of the curricula. Short refresher courses and special training of two to three weeks

complete the program. At the time of Dr. Waidelich's
visit, only about 100 students were registered in all
three schools, excluding those enrolled in local
courses in different parts of the country. The report criticizes a certain defect in training for
membership education, but finds that the theoretical
curriculum is complete, including even the historical
and international aspects of the cooperative movement.

Nigeria's educational system corresponds to the
relatively high standing of its cooperative movement
in general. Its cooperative superiority--in comparison to not only Niger but also most other African
countries--is apparently due to the continuity of
development and indicates the significance of the
government's attitude toward the colonial past.
Where nationalism prevails, and everything stemming
from the pre-independence era is abolished, not only
are institutions destroyed, but detestation and mistrust of modern ideas and methods eradicate successful earlier stages of confidence and open-mindedness,
and a new start is required in every respect. The
absence of destructive nationalism in Nigeria is not
due to the government alone. It is, to a large degree, the consequence of the administrative methods
applied by the British Government during the protectorate, methods that caused much less resentment than
the colonial administrations of other powers in Africa.

East Pakistan. The Comilla experiment is an
outstanding example of an independent cooperative
development. Its success is largely based on the
educational methods applied in reorganizing the district's cooperative societies, which, until then,
had been rather inactive. The Indian professor
A. F. A. Hussain reported to the International Cooperative Alliance in March, 1964, on the training
center, established with governmental help in the
Comilla district about three years after the beginning of the reorganization. Cooperative societies
were admitted to the reform program under certain
conditions. Emphasis was placed on weekly membership
meetings for educational purposes held under the
center's supervision. The members had to agree to

attend the meetings regularly for several years.
Many members also attended separate training courses,
which they reported on at the weekly membership meetings. In this way, more than 5,000 cooperators were
indirectly reached by the course work. All aspects
of rural life were the topics of course study and
discussion. Particular stress was laid on cooperative discipline as the prerequisite for an effective
application of the new agricultural techniques that
were taught in the courses, as well as for the success of the reform program in general. The considerable increase in the district's agricultural production after the first years of reorganization are, in
Professor Hussain's opinion, due to the educational
efforts combined with the reform program.

The Comilla experiment extended its educational
work beyond the adult and professional education
given by the training center. All cooperative members agreed to send their children to school and to
guarantee their regular attendance. Moreover, the
school lessons were adapted to the program of rural
reorganization. This was accomplished by extending
promotion and information on all phases of the reform to two extremely influential groups in the pop-
ulation--the women and the village priests (imams).
Both groups were taught the basic ideas of the reform program, with the emphasis mainly on the principles of cooperative work and the cooperative way
of life.

The report expresses the conviction that the
education of the women and the village priests def-
initely contributed to the success of the Comilla
experiment. It quotes the judgment of the director
of the Pakistani Academy for Rural Development, who
characterized the outcome of the reform as equally
beneficial to the cooperative movement of the region,
to general education, and to the women's status.

The Comilla experiment was performed in the
least developed sector of East Pakistan. But it had
the advantage of being supported by the Training
Center and the Academy, which had been established
before the experiment was initiated and were of great

help to the organizers of the reform program. Where
no such institutions exist and cooperative education
has to break new ground, extraordinary efforts are
required.

This is reflected in several reports on Uganda,
a British protectorate that became independent in
1962. These reports are combined and condensed below. The first report (undated, but apparently issued in 1962 or later) is part of a presentation by
the Cooperative League of America, and is entitled
"Co-ops in Africa--The Need for Peace Corps Co-op
Teams." A second report is by John M. Eklund, the
Director of the National Farmers Union Department
for Cooperative Development. This was issued after
his study tour through various Asian and African
countries in 1963. Two additional reports were presented to the International Cooperative Training
Center in Madison, Wisconsin, in 1963 and 1964 by
native cooperative leaders from Uganda. A final report is contained in the National Farmers Union publication "Partners in Development Around the World."
This last was issued in June, 1964, together with a
survey of the initial results of cooperative education in Uganda.

Unsuccessful efforts by the Uganda Government
to reduce the dominating role of reckless traders
and to overcome rural resistance to cooperative organizations convinced the country's leaders of the
need of foreign aid to cooperative education. They
first applied for help to the Loughborough Cooperative College in England and subsequently to American
cooperative organizations. A number of British experts came to the country, and a group of American
advisers started to work there in November, 1963.
Educational institutions were established on three
different levels: regional centers for employees'
training started courses with 300 participants; education of members by centrally trained teaching personnel was initiated in more than 300 villages;
finally, the employees and workers of a formerly unsuccessful cooperative marketing center were systematically trained for jobs on all levels of the
organization.

All reports show that the greatest obstacle to
cooperative education was the Ugandians themselves.
Solidarity, responsibility, and other basic requirements of cooperative work were unknown ideas to most
of the people. One report pointed out the difficulty
in interesting the people in working habits and methods that would increase their income. A later report
expressed doubts as to whether educational results
would last after a less cooperative-minded government came to power. This report, presented by a native cooperative leader, discussed the country's political instability and its eventual impact on cooperative progress. Two years later, however, the
combined efforts of the government and the American
advisers showed considerable results. More than
5,000 leaders of local cooperatives, about 500 managers of central organizations, and 200 instructors
for rural districts had successfully finished their
training courses by the end of 1964. Sufficient
teaching materials and textbooks in the native language were available. Trucks equipped with film cam-
eras visited all parts of the country to promote and
explain cooperative methods to villagers. The American
organizers and leaders of these various educational
efforts worked with great patience, carefully adapting to the conditions and capacities of the population. Also, American sources provided generous investments and contributions. As a result, the final
report spoke of the over-all positive reaction to
cooperative establishments in most parts of the country. One observed that the Uganda success is important as evidence of the possibility of educating
along cooperative lines the population of a country
in which all the psychological and material prerequisites of the movement have to be imported. This
is in contrast to countries such as India, and Pakistan, where traditional and new forces form a foundation for progressive developments along cooperative
lines. This statement points to the idea of a universal program of cooperative education as conceived
by many cooperative leaders in the Western world.

A series of publications issued by the Cooperative Department of the Pan American Union deals with
educational matters in the Latin American countries.

The head of the Department, F. Chaves, with whom the
author had an opportunity to discuss at some length
cooperative developments in Latin America, added to
this material much valuable information based on his
numerous visits to the regions under review.

Assistance to cooperative movements and in
building new cooperative institutions is an essential
part of the United States' contribution to the socioeconomic improvement of the Latin American countries.
The prominent role of CUNA, in connection with the
AID programs, in helping cooperatives has been mentioned repeatedly in the foregoing chapters. CUNA's
articles in its journal Credit Union Magazine report
regularly on Latin American credit-union activities,
with emphasis on the educational value of the growing movement.

However, the cooperative education resulting
from membership in credit unions or from the efforts
of local or regional leaders to establish credit
unions or similar cooperative groups does not provide
the large-scale cooperative education necessary to
prepare greater parts of the population to free themselves from poverty, exploitation, and subjection to
unjust social conditions.

With regard to the broader aspects of cooperative education--the teaching of self-help, confidence,
social awareness, good work habits--the representatives of various agencies interested in Latin American developments seemed to agree, until recently,
that much still needs to be done. A report given by
M. A. Abrahamsen, Farmer Cooperative Service of the
U.S. Department of Agriculture, published in the
September, 1964, issue of the Service's official journal, News for Farmer Cooperatives, deals with the
cooperative movement in Brazil. Mr. Abrahamsen participated in a South American inspection tour as a
member of a group of experts appointed by AID. Brazil
then had more than 5,000 cooperative societies--
2,000 in the agricultural sector, the remaining 3,000
mostly consumer cooperatives. The report emphasized
the need for improved membership education. One of
the main faults found during the tour was the members'

failure to comprehend the responsibilities involved
in joining a cooperative society.

The same point was stressed at the conference
of Latin American consumer cooperatives in Puerto
Rico (June, 1963). The president of the Organization
of the Cooperatives of America, L. A. Suarez, called
for expanded educational programs, embracing all
facets of the cooperative movement and coordinating
the existing individual institutions and workshops
with the curricula established by CUNA, the Cooperative League, and the organization of consumer cooperatives.

A group of cooperative leaders in Latin American
countries recently drew up a list of educational
postulates as the result of their joint deliberations
on necessary improvements. This document holds that
cooperative ideas and principles should be communi-
cated not only to those professionally interested,
but to everybody as part of general education. The
curricula of elementary and high schools, of teachers' colleges and universities, should include cooperative matters. The promotion of school cooperatives, the addition of cooperative instruction to the
community development programs, and the establishment of model cooperative societies as media of education are also called for. Some of these goals
have been realized over the last years, although
mainly only by individual institutions and not as
generally accepted, compulsory regulations. Among
the first institutions to add cooperative instruction to their programs were the University of Puerto
Rico, the National University of La Plata (Argentina),
the Central American University in Tegucigalpa (Honduras), and the Brazilian State University in São
Paulo.

There is widespread recognition among the cooperative leaders of Latin American states that the
proliferation of cooperative institutions in most
parts of the region has not been accompanied by the
appropriate means of education. This recognition is
encouraging for the role of cooperation in the continuing struggle for socioeconomic and political

progress and stability in these countries.

An educational center of growing importance to
developing countries has originated from the "Antigonish Movement" in Canada. In the early 1920's,
St. Francis University in Antigonish, Canada, began
to form peasants, fishermen, miners, and other laborers in the eastern provinces of the country into
small groups. Originally this was done for general
educational purposes, but later they were organized
along professional lines for the attainment of better working conditions. These groups evolved into
peasant, fishermen, and workmen cooperatives for
credit, supply, and insurance, and eventually spread
over larger areas. St. Francis University established a special institute in 1959 for the international promotion of the Antigonish principles, particularly the education of cooperative leaders.
Theoretical and practical instructions are combined
in courses of eight months, and include all kinds of
cooperative activities. Over the last few years,
international organizations have increasingly begun
to grant stipends to social workers and cooperative
leaders in developing countries to study in Antigonish. The school is now an internationally acknowledged center of cooperative education for emerging
areas.

The reference to Antigonish leads to a short
consideration of cooperative education offered in
the United States and Europe for developing countries.
Some educational institutions in Western countries
where foreign cooperative leaders are trained have
already been mentioned. Few have a long tradition
in this field. Until after World War II, cooperative
education was of actual interest to the colonial
powers only. The British Cooperative College, the
Plunkett Foundation for Cooperative Studies in London, the French Collège Coopératif, and the Centre
International de la Coopération in Paris, are important in this connection. Their educational work was
based on the colonial status of the respective areas
and oriented to the cooperative traditions and interests of the colonial power. Cooperative education
was directed less toward progress in general and more

toward organizing the work of natives to improve the
yield and to establish discipline among rural workers.   But we have seen that these aims are not irreconcilable with the general goals of cooperative education, and that, for example, in India, Nigeria,
and other former British colonies and protectorates,
new cooperative institutions were built on foundations
laid in colonial times.   The French and Belgian cooperative ventures were less successful and often led
to strong resentment and mistrust of new cooperative
initiatives of any kind.

Modern educational efforts were based on recognition that the cooperative methods of organization
are among the most effective means for technical and
spiritual progress, paving the way to socioeconomic
improvements and political independence.

With this idea in mind, numerous private and
semiprivate organizations in the United States and
Europe began, in the early 1950's, to invite cooperators from developing countries to visit their
institutions and to participate in training courses.
These invitations were usually combined with (or led
to corresponding applications from the visitors for)
the assignment of American or European experts as
educators and teachers to foreign countries.   With
great idealism and large investments of material and
intellectual capital, cooperative organizations,
welfare institutions, churches, industrial associations, and other interested groups began to contribute to cooperative developments in various regions
and to organize training opportunities abroad and
at home.   Because of inadequate preparation, insufficient funds, and often an overemphasis on technical factors and neglect of the human and social aspects, some of these undertakings had disappointing
results.   In many cases, and usually through trial
and error, an adjustment to the complexity of the
problems involved was achieved.   A certain coordination, at least within individual countries, led to
more systematic and effective actions.

The International Cooperative Development Service of the U.S. Agency for International Development,

the German Foundation for Developing Countries in
cooperation with the Joint Committee of German Cooperative Associations, cooperative centers in Sweden,
Holland, Switzerland, and other European countries
helped organize and coordinate aid to developing
countries, specifically in education. International
agencies, especially the FAO, ILO, United Nations,
the International Cooperative Alliance, IFAP, the
OECD, coordinated their work with the activities of
individual countries. The conference reports in
Chapter 6 and "Coordinating Aid to Cooperative Movements in Developing Countries" at the end of this
book refer in particular to these matters. The present chapter concerns some essential improvements that
characterize cooperative education in and for developing countries in recent years.

Despite the many different educational programs
offered by both permanent and transitory institutions
in nearly all Western countries, certain common trends
can be traced in the endless stream of publications on
cooperative work in developing countries and related
educational problems. Without claiming to cover the
whole field and aware of his possibly one-sided view,
the author believes that three realizations characterize recent trends in the educational programs:

1) Cooperative establishments, laws, and regulations of the Western nations are no longer presented to emerging populations as directives or
models, but only as examples of the accomplishments
attained under the individual conditions of a particular country. The politico-historical and socioeconomic developments that determine cooperative
movements are emphasized.

2) Technical training, including organizational,
administrative, and financial, must be accompanied
and often preceded by ideological and spiritual education on all levels of cooperative instruction.

3) Experts and advisers assigned to cooperative
work in developing countries must be selected carefully and thoroughly prepared for the specifics of
their assignment, the country's conditions, and all

data related to their imminent duties, even if they are experienced specialists in their native country.

A few examples demonstrate these conclusions:

1) The International Cooperative Training Center in Madison, Wisconsin, states in its general directory that "cooperatives cannot be successfully operated or understood out of context," and that the aim of the Center's training methods is "to encourage independent thinking, decision-making and action."

2) The international courses for cooperative leaders from developing countries offered by the cooperative school in Stuttgart-Hohenheim, Germany, organized by the Joint Committee of German Cooperative Associations, are regularly open to participants from regions or groups of developing countries who speak the same language or have the same traditional or religious bonds or are neighbors. This is in order to tailor the courses to the specifics of each region or group.

3) The Fourth Annual Report to the Congress on Technical and Economic Assistance to Cooperative Enterprises, dated March 21, 1966, prepared by the International Cooperative Development Service of the Agency for International Development, states: "The most important task for cooperative technicians and advisers is to be able to communicate with the people in the villages and countryside about things they are interested in, in ways that they can understand."

4) The leader of several international cooperative seminars of the German Foundation for Developing Countries, Professor Hans Wilbrandt, of the University of Göttingen, in summarizing the main topics of a series of lectures delivered by several international authorities on cooperative education to a group of African cooperators, stated that the common conclusion is that ideological education is at least as important as technical training.

5) The quarterly report of A. A. Bailey, Executor Director of the CUNA World Extension Department,

Madison, Wisconsin, enumerates the following courses
for Peace Corps members in preparation for their assignments to CUNA work in several countries. These
were all carried out during the last quarter 1966:

 a) Four weeks for volunteer going to Venezuela.

 b) Two weeks for a group going to Bolivia.

 c) Another course (time not indicated) for
Costa Rica.

 d) One week for volunteers going to Bechuanaland.

 e) One course for a group assigned to Jamaica.

Altogether this is 230 hours spent in Peace Corps
training programs.

 6) In 1962, the author attended a meeting at
the German Central Association of Rural Cooperatives
(Deutscher Raiffeisenverband) in Bonn, Germany, where
selected members of the organization were trained to
be cooperative educators in Asian and African countries. The main focus of the meeting was a report
given by a man who had just returned from a similar
assignment to Afghanistan, where he had spent two
years in different rural districts working with cooperative institutions. He stressed the need for
careful preparation for individual conditions in different regions and the importance of adaptation to
regional traditions and habits.

 These few references to the similar programs,
but substantially different concepts of the prerequisites, goals, and principles of cooperative education
in developing countries demonstrate the progressive
methods characterized by the new educational tendencies. They are in accord with the repeatedly cited
ILO report on the role of cooperatives in developing
countries, namely that education and systematic research, based on practical experience, must be combined in order to enlarge and improve the knowledge
required to build effective cooperative movements in
these poor regions.

CHAPTER **6** COOPERATIVE AID TO
DEVELOPING COUNTRIES

The years 1965 and 1966 were marked by a number
of international and regional conferences and meetings of specific significance to cooperative developments in developing countries. The reports clearly
reflect the increasing consideration given to the
ideas under review in this book. Cooperators in developed as well as in developing countries seem to
recognize more than ever before the many-sided pre-
sumptions and involvements of cooperative establishments in the framework of social, cultural, and economic progress.

In contrast to the foregoing chapters, each of
which referred to a particular sector of cooperative
work, this chapter discusses the many different aspects set forth during the most important recent conferences. The objectives and participants in these
meetings were very diverse, although the basic ideas
had considerable similarities.

The author does not attempt to present a complete chronicle of all such events. Moreover, no
other sources of information were at his disposal.
Nonetheless, the main trends of the work in progress
are sufficiently shown in the conference reports
described below:

1) The International Labor Conferences, Geneva,
Switzerland, June, 1965, and June, 1966, in so far
as they are concerned with cooperation.

2) The Fifth Far East Agricultural Credit and
Cooperative Workshop, Seoul, Korea, May, 1965.

3) The International Confederation of Agricultural Credit Meeting, Tunis, Tunisia, October, 1965.

4) The Fourth African Conference on the Mobilization of Local Savings, Nairobi, Kenya, December, 1965.

5) The FAO Regional Seminar on Cooperative Farming, New Delhi, India, May, 1966.

6) The Second Inter-American Conference of Ministers of Labor, Carabella Parish, Venezuela, May, 1966.

7) The Seventh Cooperative Seminar of the International Cooperative Training Center, Madison, Wisconsin, January-June, 1966.

8) The World Land Reform Conference, FAO Headquarters, Rome, Italy, June-July, 1966.

9) The First International Conference on Cooperative Assistance to Developing Countries, Fredensborg, Denmark, September, 1965.

10) The First International Conference of the Major Cooperative Thrift and Credit Organizations, Jamaica, October, 1966.

THE INTERNATIONAL LABOR CONFERENCES
(Geneva, Switzerland, 1965 and 1966)

The ILO recommendation in 1963 of rules for the establishment of cooperatives and their working conditions in developing countries has been mentioned in Chapter 2, and the initial ILO report on this ("The Role of Cooperatives in the Economic and Social Development of Developing Countries") has been cited repeatedly in the foregoing chapters. Because of the decisive character of the 1965 Plenary Session of the ILO with regard to the planned action, some of this conference's main topics, preliminaries, and results are described in the following paragraphs.

The Committee on Cooperatives of the 49th Session of the International Labor Conference met in June, 1965, and discussed the proposed document and answers received from seventy-four member countries to the questionnaire that had been sent with the above-mentioned ILO report. Some highlights of the discussions may be seen in the following statements. They show the general consent to the publication of a document according to the ILO recommendations, although there were pronounced differences. These were to be expected in view of the varied composition of the committee, which included representatives of government administrations, employers' organizations, and employees and workers from both Western and Eastern countries.

Representatives of developing countries pointed out that "there were no major sociological obstacles to the further growth of cooperatives which had a long tradition in many developing countries and bore marked affinities to closely knit tribal and community structures that had prevailed since an early date." Added, however, was the comment that "there were in some instances psychological barriers of an individual and collective nature that had to be surmounted when new concepts took the place of traditional values."

The committee members representing labor unions wanted the planned document to give more emphasis to the interrelationship of trade unions and unions of cooperatives. Representatives of employers' organizations stressed the important role that cooperatives could play in efforts toward economic and social progress, but only if the fundamental criteria of cooperation--"voluntary nature of the association, democratic control and independence of the cooperative"--were guaranteed.

A number of committee members wanted more emphasis on cooperatives' contribution to "improving conditions of living of the population as a whole," mainly in agrarian reforms. Others stressed the social and educational significance of cooperative work and its role in "developing other facets of the human personality apart from the purely economic."

Members of all groups agreed that there was a need for "governmental promotion, assistance and supervision of cooperatives, but these should be of temporary nature, . . . and cooperatives should be allowed to stand on their own feet . . . as soon as they were able . . . to do so."

The director of the International Cooperative Alliance addressed the committee on behalf of his organization and of the International Federation of Agricultural Producers. A representative of the FAO also made a statement. The former emphasized the value of cooperatives "in their capacity to change negative habits and attitudes of mind and to develop human potentialities to the full." The latter drew attention to "the need for government assistance in cooperative development in certain countries, especially as regards finance," and underlined the need for coordination with the FAO and ILO aid to cooperative movements.

The committee then began an examination of the "Proposed Conclusions," as outlined in the ILO Report VII (2).

The majority were opposed to giving the projected instrument the form of a "Convention." It was decided to call it "Proposed Recommendations." Several amendments to the original draft of the first part of the document defining the "scope" of cooperative activities were proposed and partly accepted. The final text to be presented to the ensuing Plenary Meeting was agreed upon as follows:

> This Recommendation applies to all categories of cooperatives, including consumer cooperatives, land-improvement cooperatives, agricultural productive and processing cooperatives, rural-supply cooperatives, agricultural-marketing cooperatives, fishery cooperatives, service cooperatives, handicraft cooperatives, workers' productive

cooperatives, labor-contracting cooperatives, cooperative thrift and credit
societies and banks, housing cooperatives,
transport cooperatives, mutual-insurance
cooperatives and health cooperatives.

This list reflects the Conference's desire not to
exclude any type of cooperative society from the
principles stated in the Recommendations. It also
shows the emphasis on improving labor conditions in
developing countries through cooperative organizations. This concern explains the mention of consumer
cooperatives first in the above text, in spite of the
statement made by the ILO in the preparatory brochure,
Report VII (1), 1964. According to this statement,
"consumers' cooperation is likely to be the last
rather than the first form of cooperation to be initiated" in developing countries.

Certain compromises between conflicting opinions
of the committee members may have contributed to the
framing of the definition of the "scope" of cooperative activities. This is mainly in regard to cooperative production, which is taken into consideration
by adding the adjective "productive" to "processing"
in the agricultural field, and by listing "workers'
productive cooperatives" among the different categories. These rather short references to cooperative forms of production suggest a certain reluctance
on the part of some committee members to extend a
cooperative program to productive fields in recognition of the aspects of this problem as outlined in
Chapter 3 of this book.

The placing of "cooperative thrift and credit
societies and banks" near the end of the list, although all ILO members are probably familiar with
the leading role of appropriate savings and loan
institution in the establishment of cooperative organizations in developing countries, was possibly a
concession to participants from Communist countries,
where self-financed associations are not desired.

An interesting result of the committee discussions of Part 2 of the proposed recommendations was

an amendment suggesting that 1) the objectives concerning cooperatives should cover a wider field than
economic and social development and also extend to
include human advancement. This appeal to enlarge
the original text came from the representative of a
Middle Eastern government, and was generally approved
by adding the words "cultural development" and "human" to the paragraph, which now reads:

> The establishment and the growth of coop-
> eratives should be regarded as one of the
> important instruments for economic, social
> and cultural development as well as human
> advancement in developing countries.

After thirteen days of deliberation, the committee agreed upon the "Proposed Conclusions," to be
presented to the Plenary Sessions, where the draft
was on the agenda for June 22, 1965. A delegate from
Sweden acted as reporter, and pointed to the remarkable degree of unanimity that had characterized the
committee's work. Delegates from Lebanon, the United
Arab Republic, and Mauritania, as chairman and vice
chairmen of the committee, gave additional explanations of the recommended text. Except for some minor
criticism, a large number of Plenary Session members
from all parts of the world consented to the action
under consideration and acknowledged the ILO staff's
careful preparation of the Recommendations and the
diligent work of the Committee. The main objections
came from the Russian delegate, and were based upon
his political ideas of "cooperation," as was to be
expected.

He wanted more emphasis on "the role of cooperatives in the eradication of the consequences of
colonialism and of the need to do away with the un-
fair terms of trade that have been practiced by cap-
italist monopolies vis-à-vis developing countries."
He regretted the "undue attention to financial aid
provided directly to cooperatives from private
sources." He pointed to "the paramount role of
producer-cooperatives, as they placed the means of
production, the basis of every country's economy, on
a socialized basis." These critical remarks, however,

did not prevent the Russian delegate from finally
consenting to the proposed instrument, which he characterized as an "acceptable basis for further discussion."

The 1965 Plenary Session of the International
Labor Conference then adopted the Committee's report
and the proposed conclusions unanimously. The five
chapters of the document, with an appendix on specific aspects of "various forms of cooperatives in
the successful implementation of agrarian reform,"
provide an historic statement that should be studied
carefully by everybody interested in cooperative work
in developing countries.

That the ILO did not draw up an actual international "Convention" but merely issued "Recommendations" is certainly advantageous to future adjustments
to changing conditions, which otherwise would be hampered by more binding rules and regulations.

In order to become an official ILO decision,
the document decided upon at the 1965 Plenary Session
had to be presented again to the ensuing session. On
June 21, 1966, the ILO decided at its Fiftieth Plenary
Session to adopt as "Recommendation 127" the proposed
document. The introductory paragraph of the meeting's
minutes states that the document "may be cited as the
Cooperative (Developing Countries) Recommendation,
1966."

A comparison of the final document, called the
"Authentic Text" (in English and French), with the
proposed text prepared at the 1965 ILO Conference
shows a number of minor, mostly formal adjustments.
But three additions to the 1965 text seem to be
characteristic of the increasing trend to emphasize
the democratic principles of cooperation, the need
for special legislation adapted to the "special conditions" under which cooperatives function, and the
necessity to apply methods of training and education
that are individually adapted to a particular area's
cultural conditions. Thus, these last-minute amendments seek to avoid schematism in cooperative work
and to give attention to the sociological and

psychological conditions that prevail in every individual region and specific case.

The three textual changes are:

1) Under "Objectives of Policy Concerning Cooperatives," a subparagraph 3(c) has been inserted that
describes cooperatives as media for "contributing to
the economy an increased measure of democratic control of economic activity and of equitable distribution of surplus."

2) Under "Methods of Implementation of Policy
Concerning Cooperatives," Part 1 on "Legislation," a
subparagraph 10(c) has been added recommending the
adoption of "fiscal laws and regulations to the special conditions of cooperatives."

3) Part 2 of the same chapter on "Education and
Training" shows an amendment to paragraph 19(3) regarding "special programs of practical training,"
adding to the original text the recommendation that
"these programs should take into account local cultural conditions, and the need to disseminate literacy and knowledge of elementary arithmetic."

THE FIFTH FAR EAST AGRICULTURAL CREDIT
AND COOPERATIVE WORKSHOP
(Seoul, Korea, May, 1965)

The Workshop was held May 10-22, 1965, according to the program established at the first meeting
of this kind in 1956, in Manila. At that time, the
delegates had agreed upon "biannual meetings to be
held so that participating countries could periodi-
cally assess what improvements had been made in agriculture, particularly in the fields of credit and
cooperatives."

The 1965 Workshop was the largest since 1956,
attended by fifty-one delegates and an almost equal
number of observers. The delegates were from Taiwan,
Japan, South Korea, the Philippines, Thailand, South
Vietnam, and the Ryukyu Islands. In addition to

observers from the same countries, the following international organizations and foreign agencies were represented:

1) Afro-Asian Rural Reconstruction Organization
2) Cooperative League of the U.S.A.
3) FAO
4) International Cooperative Alliance
5) Economic Commission for Asia and the Far East.
6) Agency for International Development

AID had been the sponsor of all four preceding workshops. It was characterized, in the 1965 report, as having moved "from sponsorship to active cooperation."

In addition to this active United States participation, several American observers accompanied some of the country delegations, and Dr. John M. Eklund, the Director of the International Assistance Corporation (National Farmers Union), Washington, D.C., acted as the official Workshop consultant.

The Workshop divided itself into five separate groups:

1) Assistance for Rural Development
2) Effective Rural Credit
3) Improving Cooperative Resources
4) Comparative Cooperative Structures
5) Education and Training

Each group prepared a report that was presented to one of the last Plenary Meetings.

In the Plenary Sessions, each delegation presented its country's report on developments since the previous workshop. In addition, a number of major papers were read in different Plenary Sessions under the following headings, with delegates from two different countries reporting separately on each of the topics below:

Credit Delinquency
Village Cooperatives

Education and Training
Capital Mobilization
Elements of Success
Land Resources

An extraordinarily well-composed report, prepared and edited under the direction of an AID consultant and a representative of the U.S. Operations
Mission to Korea, sets forth the activities and results of the Workshop. It contains highly valuable
documentations of the efforts made and progress
achieved in agricultural cooperation in the Far East.
It also shows the continuing difficulties that seem
to prevail equally in all seven countries represented
at the Workshop. These difficulties indicate the
hard road ahead for most developing countries in their
efforts to apply cooperative methods to their agricultural conditions.

Some of the Workshop's most characteristic comments appear in the following paragraphs. They are
concerned mainly with social and individual factors,
which form the background of a number of reports
given by the delegates and other participants.

"The Role of Rural Savings" was discussed at the
opening session by Dr. Joel Bernstein, director of
the U.S. Operations Mission to Korea. He pointed to
the cooperative form of organization as most suitable
for the accumulation of investment capital. Also,
he underlined the cooperative members' participation
in decision-making as "one of the finest examples of
training for responsible citizenship," invoking "a
type of mutual responsibility which tends toward the
highest common denominator of group judgment."

The next speaker at the opening ceremony was
Dr. Eklund, the consultant to the Workshop, whose
theme was "Credit and Cooperatives as Economic Instruments." He discussed, among many other problems,
the initial role of governments in establishing cooperative movements. He reported on his work with
more than a dozen developing countries and their
over-all tendency to effect an early practical with-
drawal of direct government control as the main

prerequisite for bringing the human values into full effect. "The human values in cooperation cannot be overestimated. . . . Cooperators are taking the first step toward economic independence. . . . The cooperative frequently becomes a community center and the base for community and village improvement by widening its functions and activity." Dr. Eklund concluded by saying, "Cooperatives are human institutions admirably suited to perform the tasks individuals cannot do for themselves," such as "income improvement, institution building and human development."

In view of Dr. Eklund's leading role as the Workshop's permanent consultant, his remarks may be seen as an expression of ideas that were dominant in the Workshop's deliberations.

The Korean Vice Minister and President of the Government's Economic Planning Board, Hak Yul Kim, outlined the basic objectives of his country's Economic Development Plan and the role of agricultural cooperatives in that plan. Among the obstacles to be overcome with the help of cooperative organizations, he said, was the "lack in economic ethics." Toward this end, "the government has organized agricultural cooperatives to strengthen agricultural activities and take measures to eliminate usurious moneylending."

Similar remarks on the necessity and expectation of abolishing usury were made in nearly every report. In all Far Eastern countries, the farmers' survival is still endangered by the calamity of usurious debts, and the fight against usury is one of the strongest forces behind the establishment of cooperative savings and credit institutions. A delegate of the Philippines described the small farmers' condition in his country:

> The farmer tends to take a fatalistic rather than a manipulative attitude toward the improvement of his lot. Rather than try to do something to shape his own destiny, he passively accepts things as they come, leaving

it to God, to the government, to the poli-
ticians, to anyone else but himself to determine his future. The interplay of all these
factors and conditions--economic, political,
cultural, physical, etc.--results in his
being caught in the web of a vicious cycle
(low productivity--low income--low savings--
poor technology--and back to low productivity), from which he can hardly extricate
himself. Agricultural credit and cooperatives are one of the means that can be effectively used to break this vicious cycle.

To this end, the Philippine National Cooperative
Bank and the Philippine Cooperative Credit Union
League have been established. Considerable aid has
been granted by AID and by the League's affiliation
with CUNA International in Madison, Wisconsin. Technical assistance from the ILO also helps the Philippines to build cooperatives to alleviate the still
poor conditions of the farmers' work and life.

The Workshop report from Japan on "Progress in
Cooperatives and Credit" starkly presented a dilemma
that also vexes many highly developed countries in
the West--the discrepancy between the general economic progress and the relative backwardness of the
agricultural sector. During the ten years ending in
1963, Japan's total economy expanded two and a half
times, at an annual rate of close to 10 per cent,
due to the country's rapid industrial reconstruction.
Agricultural income at the beginning of this period
had been 18 per cent of the total national income,
but by the end of the ten years it had dropped to
about 9 per cent. The marked disparity between the
primary industries (agriculture and raw materials)
and the finished-goods industries, including export,
prompted the government to design a new plan at the
end of 1964. Its objective was to achieve more sta-
bilized conditions, mainly by forcing improvements
in the agricultural structure. Included in the plan
was an increase in agricultural cooperative funds
and related operations. The final paragraph of the
Japanese report states that "agricultural cooperative financing is pre-eminent in the amounts of

agricultural credit-giving business. Government banking institutions are playing the functions in giving
exclusively long-term and low-interest rate credits,
while general-purpose banking institutions give
short-term credits only." This statement clearly defines the different approaches to agricultural financing from cooperatives, the government, and banks,
emphasizing the "pre-eminent" role of cooperative
credit.

Cooperatives originated in Japan in 1900, but
were, according to the report, "kept in abeyance during wartime." That remark understates the stagnation of genuine cooperative work under dictatorial
conditions, such as prevailed in Japan during periods
of militarism.

The 1964 plan tries to find solutions to the
four "major agricultural problems":

1) to develop a type of "economically viable
   farmer"

2) to maintain the country's "food self-
   sufficiency"

3) to stabilize the prices of farm and livestock products

4) to cope with the requirements of import
   liberalization

The fourth point is of paramount importance.
Since 1964, Japan has been categorized by the International Monetary Fund as a country obligated to
liberalize its import regulations. This has resulted
in additional overseas competition, especially in the
already vulnerable sector of agriculture.

After describing the main weaknesses of Japan's
agriculture (small holdings of cultivated land, rural
population flow into nonagricultural jobs, increasing production costs), the report sets forth the government's expectation that agricultural cooperatives
will help to solve some of the most urgent problems,

especially with regard to appropriate means of credit
administration. To this end, credit to farmers shall
be reorganized to be more "closely connected with
their farm business management and their daily life."
The credit management of individual cooperative societies shall "back up the economic federations of
agricultural cooperatives in order that the latter
may make an inroad into farm commodity markets."

This seems to point to a dominant role for cooperative federations in regulating market prices.
If the credit policies of individual cooperative societies would thus become subordinate to the federations' programs, a conflict could arise between the
cooperatives own credit policies and the federation's
adherence to the government program of price stabilization. This problem may be solved in "study meetings" announced in the delegate's report. The Japanese Ministry of Agriculture and Forestry plans to
arrange these meetings to prepare the reform program
with all interested parties, including representatives
of the agricultural cooperative movement.

The delegation from South Vietnam introduced its
report with the remark that since the previous Workshop two years ago, "the struggle against increasing
Communist infiltration and terrorism has overshadowed
all other endeavors" in its country. The agricultural
credit and cooperative program, successfully started
between 1958 and 1960, along the guidelines laid down
by previous workshops, was seriously hampered between
1960 and 1962. Against this background, the successful continuation of cooperative work in all parts of
the country where relatively normal conditions were
preserved is a remarkable fact. A considerable network of cooperative units and farmers' associations
still functions, organized by or in connection with
the National Agricultural Credit Office and the Directorate of Cooperatives. As of December 31, 1964,
more than seventy agencies and subagencies of the
Credit Office were in operation, and more than 300
local cooperative societies with about 130,000 members belonged to the Directorate. In addition,
284,000 farmers were organized in 10,000 small agricultural units plus 800 village farmers' associations

under about 100 provincial and district offices. Education and training is one of the main functions of all these units. In spite of war and revolution, 500 training courses with 23,000 participants and 71 special cooperative courses with 3,300 participants were held in the two troubled years of 1963 and 1964. The 1965-66 program has been extended, with the help of hundreds of mobile field agents contacting the rural population in remote areas. These data and the whole tenor of the report attest to the unbroken spirit of the Vietnamese cooperative leadership.

The progress report of Thailand's delegate to the Workshop referred to the five-year period since 1961, when a program of credit-service improvement was launched to strengthen the numerous small village cooperatives. New legislation has been prepared in connection with the request to amalgamate cooperative societies whose size does not allow satisfactory results. A shortage of trained personnel and a lack of coordination between agricultural credit and extension services are obstacles to be eliminated in future programs in order to reach more farmers. Until 1965, only about 8 per cent were organized in cooperative form. The majority of Thailand's farmers own small plots, and are expected to be organized cooperatively as soon as the new program is in effect.

In Korea, an amendment on cooperatives was recently added to the Constitution. The new Article 115 reads:

> The State shall encourage the development of cooperatives founded on the self-help spirit of the farmers, fishermen, and small and medium businessmen, and shall guarantee their political impartiality.

This one sentence combines the principles of self-help and political neutrality with the statement of governmental initiative in cooperative movements. It is a classic expression of cooperative policies required in developing countries.

Korea has also tried to merge small village cooperatives into larger units. Its program aimed to

reduce the present 21,500 units to about 8,000 by
1967, each with a membership of at least 200 farmers.
However, the merger program did not reach its goal
for the first period. Instead of the 15,500 cooperative units aimed for by 1964, there were will
19,000. The report mentions "great socioeconomic
difficulties" in this connection, and points to the
problem of combining the principle of cooperative
self-government with practical requirements from
above.

The cooperative leaders in Korea found that a
uniform program did not work. They divided the cooperative societies into three categories with separate programs. Category A is for societies with
good management, a complete bookkeeping system, and
members who generally understood the methods of joint
purchasing and marketing operations. The program
for this category centers around the improvement of
farm management and development of ways for the farmers to supplement their income through off-farm
work. Category B covers cooperatives with the potential to attain Category A standards but still needing
training and guidance that a specific program can
perform. Category C cooperatives have insufficiently
educated members, poor leadership, and poor records.
Their reorganization program starts at the bottom
and embraces all aspects of cooperative work.

In spite of a hopeful beginning, the threefold
program met with difficulties, characterized in the
report as a consequence of business expansion accompanied by growing resistance against outside influences and criticism. This explanation coincides with
similar experiences in Western countries, and reminds
the author of the difficult period of the 1920's,
when the German agricultural cooperative movement had
to be reorganized, against considerable resistance
in the cooperative ranks, despite the urgent need to
avoid disintegration. The Korean Government is hopeful of overcoming resistance with the help of enlarged training facilities, which AID, the FAO, and
the ILO are expected to support.

The Ryukyu Islands, an archipelago extending

374 miles in the West Pacific between Taiwan in the
southwest and Japan in the northeast, comprise sixty-
four islands, forty-eight of which are inhabited.
They were part of the Japanese Empire until the end
of World War II. In 1945, they were placed under a
U.S. Military Governor, now the U.S. Civil Administration of the Ryukyu Islands. Of the islands' 850
square miles of total land area, only 25 per cent
are arable, and they support 74,000 farm families,
representing about one-third of the total population.
The average size of the farms is less than one hectare.

From 1955 through 1963, the islands experienced
a considerable growth of economic income. Agricultural progress, however, is far behind industrial
development. A large number of the agricultural and
fishery cooperatives are employed to channel credits
from the Central Bank of the country to farmers,
fishermen, and others.

The underemployed part of the farm population
will, under the economic program in action, be ab-
sorbed by industrial projects now under consideration.
The help to fully active farmers will be concentrated on structural improvements. Small owners will be
encouraged to join large-scale farming units. This
program is combined with a technical modernization
program and with efforts to improve the agricultural
credit system, mainly through cooperation. The Central Bank dispenses considerable capital funds for
agricultural modernization. These funds are partly
from cooperative sources, since the cooperatives
share in the Central Bank's authorized capital, as
prescribed by a 1963 law. The short time elapsed
since then is apparently the reason for the absence
of detailed data of progress reached in the Ryukyu
Islands at the time of the Workshop meeting.

The major papers presented to the Workshop, in
addition to individual country reports, gave some
aspects of specific importance to the sociological
and psychological sides of cooperative work. A representative of the Central Bank of the Philippines,
referring to credit delinquency, went back to the

"deep-rooted characteristics of [his country's] ar-
chaic land-tenure system . . . shaped by the ancient
Malayan ancestors," when "in the pre-Spanish days,
the social structure of the village consisted of
four main classes of people--nobility, freemen, serfs,
and slaves." Remains of this structure are still
traceable in the present classification of the Philippines' agricultural population.

A study conducted several years ago showed that
16 per cent of the farmers were owners, 19 per cent
part owners, 13 per cent lessees, and 52 per cent
share-tenants. The two last groups comprise some
two-thirds of all farmers, depending completely on
their landlords, who supply most of the capital invested (about 88 per cent). Heavy dependence on
credit and little or no savings are a legacy of the
old structural order. Private moneylenders are the
principal source of credit. The report lists them,
without discrimination with regard to their ruthless
methods of exploitation, as the landlords, merchants,
storekeepers, and relatives and "friends." Interest
rates reaching as high as 300 per cent are still in
effect. The general remoteness of credit institutions accounts for the inadequacy of credit sources
needed to cope with the credit needs of the great
majority of small farmers. A low rate of repayment
is the result of these conditions and the small size
of most farms with poor productivity.

A remarkable statement in the report strongly
confirms observations made in other parts of the
world and repeatedly mentioned in earlier chapters:

> Social and cultural factors--customs and
> traditions or conventions, cultural pat-
> terns, etc.--are the basic elements of the
> sociological environments which exert a
> tremendous influence upon the effectiveness
> of agricultural credit programs.

The report gives a detailed picture of the "strong
family ties" and the obligation to help relatives,
which means that "any sort of excess is transferred
to needy relatives." This discourages farmers from

producing more than required for their own family.
Also, "the Filipino's consumption habits are primarily determined by social pressure from the neighbors."
Baptisms, weddings, and funerals "cost the rural
people in money and food a sum almost equal to their
annual earnings"; a reduction of this spending in
favor of productive investments is "almost impossible
or nearly unthinkable." Some years ago, a Philippine
Senator started a program to stop the extravagance of
the rural folk in celebrating fiestas. The effectiveness of this project still remains to be seen.

A more positive step toward reducing credit delinquency is the current program of supervised credit. The delegate concluded that every program for
improving agricultural credit and avoiding credit delinquency should place "more emphasis on the social
aspects of the farmer's life and conditions in its
basic concept."

Reporting on the same topic, the Deputy Director
General of the Credit and Marketing Cooperatives Department in the Ministry of National Development of
Thailand pointed to the individual farmer's productive capacity as the major criterion for determining
the size of loans. But these should also be given
out of recognition that "needed household expenses
fall under the productive category, as the farmer
together with his family is a main factor of production." As pointed out in an earlier chapter, the
life and work of small farmers are inseparable elements of agriculture and together form the vital substance of his productivity.

To avoid credit delinquency, especially among
small farmers, a form of security known in Thailand
as "group joint liability" is recommended. It provides for "mutual control for the punctual repayments
by all members of each group"--a pre-cooperative form
of credit administration and control. The report
did not disclose details of this system, but did refer to its application in several Asian countries,
including Japan, where the principle of "joint liability" is a part of the agricultural bylaws.

Credit delinquency caused by "factors beyond control" is an integral part of the complexity of agricultural risks. To cope with "natural hazards," the Thailand representative urged that cooperatives build up reserves in order to absorb as much as possible such "non-recovery" at their own level. Since only a few cooperatives could acquire sufficient reserves in the near future, the delegate suggested two means of public assistance: special guarantee funds to be kept in governmental hands, and crop and livestock insurance. Both methods have been applied successfully in Korea and Japan. In Korea, cooperative farm cattle and fire-insurance organizations have been established. In Japan, mutual relief associations are operating at the village level. Both institutions were highly recommended by the Thailand expert. His final recommendation was a procedure to release primary cooperative societies from the financial burdens of litigation with defaulters by providing in the cooperative laws ways for "quick and effective processes for the recovery of overdue loans." Appropriate government agencies should grant certificates as "final and conclusive proof of the arrears stated to be due therein." This method is applied in India and based on the Cooperative Societies Act of 1960.

The Act empowers the regional Registrar of Cooperative Societies to grant such certificates and to recover the amounts due "by attachment and/or sale of the property of the defaulter." This method may not be in line with cooperative self-administration, since it delegates a cooperative prerogative to a government agency and so contradicts the principles of autonomy, self-reliance, and mutual liability. However, it has the merits of "defrosting" frozen loans and releasing the cooperative societies from the burdens of taking legal steps against defaulters.

Papers on village cooperatives were presented by the Deputy Commissioner of the Department of Finance, Taiwan Provincial Government, and the chief of the Korean Ministry of Agriculture and Forestry. Both saw governmental initiative and help as an unavoidable compromise in developing countries, until

the spirit and means of self-administration are
strong enough to do away with such assistance and
control. Both reports give similar definitions of
the essence and structure of primary cooperatives
in small communities, and reflect equally, although
in different ways, the characteristics of farmer
members, which are the substance of the movement.
The development must be tailored to the members' individual qualities, needs, and potentialities. The
following criteria of successful cooperative work on
the village level were stated: members' confidence
in their own organization, their ability to discuss
among themselves their targets and goals, their understanding that the fundamental cooperative spirit
is not primarily concerned with profit, their being
free from involvement in political activities, and
their aim to make the village cooperative a center
for the achievement of better personal and productive standards of life for the whole community. Competition between cooperative societies and non-
cooperative organizations was praised as the safest
incentive for continual improvement of management
and member relationship.

        This necessarily short review of the two papers
dealing with village cooperatives fails to indicate
the stress that the two delegates put on the human
and social aspects of cooperation. Although both
speakers were high government officers, their concern
was obviously directed more toward self-administration
in cooperative work than toward government-led organization.

        In contrast, the two papers on Education and
Training, presented by delegates from Thailand and
Japan, merely summarized the well-known principles
of officers' training and added little to the foregoing observations on education. A short remark in
one of the papers dealt with membership education,
and recommended the application of a study-group
method in order to "contribute to greater understanding and appreciation of the problems of individual
members."

        Similarly, the remaining papers presented at the

Workshop ("Capital Mobilization," Japan and Korea; "Elements of Success," Taiwan and the Philippines; "Land Resources," Japan and Vietnam) were merely general surveys of the topics and presented no detailed information on the sociological and other backgrounds. Perhaps these speakers were trying not to repeat what already had been said in reports on countries. They may have chosen to concentrate on problems common to all Far Eastern countries, rather than individual conditions.

The Japanese leader stressed rural savings, promoted by village cooperatives through their immediate access to each villager, as the safest fundamental of "capital mobilization." Protective measures for cooperative depositors should generally be established in order to overcome the farmers' distrust, which seems to be an obstacle to cooperative saving in most Far Eastern countries.

A savings campaign started in Korean villages has had considerable success. It is based on the principle of bringing together groups of villagers with common social and economic interests. This campaign finally resulted in keeping the group members together permanently in a credit union of the CUNA type.

The importance of utilizing traditional habits has been mentioned in connection with the building of production cooperatives in Taiwan. The "mood of uncooperativeness" among old-fashioned farmers had to be overcome in order to reactivate a forty-year-old tea producers' association. The farmers had abandoned the association when it was unsuccessful in marketing their crop because of the uneven size of the tea leaves delivered by the farmers. Tea export depends on even, fine cuts of the leaves, a process achievable only with the use of expensive machines. After the machines were given to the disbanded association on credit, it was possible to convince the farmers that cooperation was to their advantage under certain conditions stipulated in new regulations and tailored to the individual needs of the members. Guided by the tea farmers' example,

farmers in other sectors of Taiwan agriculture applied similar methods.

The delegate from the Philippines pointed to
"simplicity of operations" as an important factor.
This component, at least at the start of cooperative
work, will hardly be contested by any practitioner,
but his conclusion that multipurpose cooperatives
are not simple enough for the beginning stages of
cooperation is debatable. Under normal conditions
in developing countries, selling and marketing work
best in cooperative establishments if combined with
credit. This is especially true where primitive
farmers have no access to the market except through
private merchants who exploit them. The Philippine
speaker reasoned that concentrating on credut unions
first, as "the least complex and most successful
form of cooperation," avoids the "failure and discouragement" often experienced in marketing and consumer societies, which have inherent functional com-
plexities. He concluded that, "like any reform
movement, cooperation cannot be expected to immediately sink into the consciousness and the ways of
people, but once it gets appreciated and makes its
mark, it becomes a way of life."

The major papers on land resources were presented by speakers from Japan and Vietnam. The former cited a government-organized society that was
established by a group of about 100 boys of fifteen
or sixteen, with some older leaders. In 1946, the
group started cultivating land on former military
grounds thirty miles east of Tokyo. The government
reorganized the group in 1949 as a Reclamation Agricultural Cooperative Society. By 1955, the original
members had all married and become independent farmers, but they continued to work with the cooperative
in order to improve their farming by joint utilization of tractors and other facilities. The group
now has 450 family members, with the husband and
wife as the most important source of labor. Other
formerly established societies were influenced by the
success of this experiment and applied similar methods
of voluntary cooperative farming.

A Vietnamese speaker on land resources stated that in his country the still-weak cooperative movement gets additional help from the government. He added that a 100 per cent cooperative organization of agricultural activities is "not in the interest of consumers"; to protect competition, private enterprise should be protected equally. Although this statement seems to be premature in view of Vietnam's early stage of cooperative development, it does correspond to the principle, established all over the world, of rejecting cooperative monopolism.

Some of the most remarkable conclusions and recommendations of the five work groups of the Fifth Far East Cooperative Workshop in Seoul, Korea, accepted by the Final Plenary Session in May, 1965, are:

1) Continuation of government aid to cooperatives is desirable on condition that "farmers be given every possible opportunity . . . to solve their own problems through their own efforts."

2) Agricultural and rural development projects initiated by governments should be turned over to cooperative operation and management whenever possible.

3) International trade agreements between cooperatives, such as those already successfully concluded between Thailand and Japan, should be encouraged.

4) The cycle "credit procurement--input--output--marketing--repayment" must be "tightened" by developing the multipurpose cooperative.

5) Cooperative federations should be established to strengthen, support, and coordinate the activities of primary cooperative societies.

6) Affiliation of national cooperative organizations with international bodies, such as ICA and CUNA, is highly desirable.

7) Incentives are required "to attract high

school and college graduates . . . to join the cooperative movement."

8) Educational programs undertaken by governmental, semigovernmental, and private organizations
should be coordinated, recognizing that "cooperative
training and education constitutes practical training in democratic processes. . . . The values of a
national cooperative movement may be considered as
practical experience in democracy itself."

The more technical and administrative proposi-
tions have been omitted. Although extremely important and well-stated, they were less indicative of
the emphasis given by the Far East cooperators to the
surrounding conditions, the human element, and the
broader aspects of cooperative developments. The
emphasis on these aspects in nearly all deliberations
proves that a maturity of concepts has been reached
since the First Far East Workshop convened in Manila
in 1956.

THE INTERNATIONAL CONFEDERATION
OF AGRICULTURAL CREDIT
(Tunis, Tunisia, October, 1965)

The meeting was specifically directed toward a
study of agricultural credit conditions in African
countries. Co-sponsor of the meeting was the National Bank of Tunisia. The conference reports give no
conclusions, but they do contain interesting information given by prominent African leaders.

The main report, given by the president of the
National Bank of Agricultural Credit of the Ivory
Coast, surveys conditions in Upper Volta, Tanganyika,
Gabon, Togo, and the Ivory Coast. Other reports were
presented by the president of the National Bank of
Agricultural Credit of Tunis, the general director of
the corresponding Institute of Morocco, and representatives of the national banks of Libya and Senegal.
Although the conference subject did not mention cooperatives, most of the reports referred to existing
or planned credit cooperatives.

The over-all tone of the reports is pessimistic. This may be partly due to the fact that the CICA is not specifically concerned with the problems of developing countries. Thus, the African leaders may have sought to impress the other members of the organization with the gap in agricultural credit facilities between developed and developing countries in order to evoke their interest in helping the African farmers.

Their arguments reflect most of the concepts that form the main subject of this book. The president of the National Bank of Agriculture of the Ivory Coast declared a "change of the African farmers' mentality" to be a basic requirement for financial progress. He referred to the disappointing experiences throughout the long period of colonialism in Ghana, the Sudan, Tunisia, Morocco, and Congo Léopoldville, where credit cooperatives and the Sociétés de Prévoyance failed to help the rural population. Only after the establishment of political independence were more promising programs developed, but they suffered from inadequate financial and administrative means.

The need to find new ways of financing the agricultural sector of African states was set forth in an interesting report that denied the applicability of "the classic guarantees" of credit under the circumstances prevailing in most African countries. The following economic and social conditions were cited in support of the statement:

1) Mortgages are prohibited by the general lack of property deeds, the low value of produce, and the absence of potential purchasers for most farm land.

2) No regulations exist in most African countries for the use of warrant-like instruments in agriculture.

3) Pledging of material is valid only where big machines such as tractors are available, and these are rarely used by African farmers.

4) In the absence of appropriate material and specialized controlling personnel, security deposits (deeds or metal) are not available.

5) Endorsements and guarantees, including the joint liability of cooperative members, are often deceptive, since the whole of a loan remains uncovered when only a portion of the members or guarantors meet their obligations.

In place of the "classic guarantees," the delegate proposed the following principle to govern the agricultural credit policy in African countries:

> Rather than insisting on the question of solvency, which supposes the integral coverage of the loan by tangible assets, they [the conditions of credit] endeavor to take as an essential criterion the capacity for repayment, which means the aptitude of the borrower to maintain his assets, increase production, pay the interest on the loan, and repay the principal without lowering the standard of living.

The delegate did not say how to ascertain this criterion, which, when attainable, would certainly make every "classic guarantee" superfluous--in developing as well as developed countries. What he had in mind is a problem under permanent discussion where agricultural credit methods are at stake. This is the eventual return to the system of purely personal credit, which, over the last decades, has been increasingly abolished. In the past, the concept of the individual or personal aptness of a borrower-- his professional qualification, his devotion to work, his honesty, and his social reputation--was the decisive factor in his credit rating, rather than substantial credit securities, pledges, and guarantees. The trend away from "personal" to "real" credit forms is a consequence of progress in Western agriculture, where most farmers have at their disposal a variety of seizable assets, and where legal, banking, and other regulations are well developed. These developments enable lenders and borrowers to manage all types of credit

securities in the best interests of both partners in
the credit business. Moreover, the growing volume
of agricultural credit in developed countries con-
fronts most banks with refinancing problems, which
are solved by rediscounting verifiable securities.

In countries that do not have most of these
circumstances and prerequisites of an intricate credit system, the application of personal-credit principles may be highly commendable if there are the
technical and educational means to lead the people
in reliable professional and private habits. Here
is the domain of cooperative efforts, which the delegate strongly recommended. He quoted an FAO report
that stated: "The administration of agricultural
credit must be part of a group of technical and hu-
manitarian activities, in such a way that it is an
integrating part of a coherent whole."

THE FOURTH AFRICAN CONFERENCE ON THE
MOBILIZATION OF LOCAL SAVINGS
(Nairobi, Kenya, December, 1965)

The first three conferences on cooperative
thrift and credit programs in African countries assembled in Dar es Salaam, Tanzania, in June, 1962;
in Lagos, Nigeria, in February, 1963; and in Kampala,
Uganda, in June, 1964. The fourth conference was
held in Nairobi, Kenya, in December, 1965. Like the
preceding conferences, it was organized by CUNA International and the United States in cooperation
with the appropriate department of the host country--
in this case, the Ministry of Cooperatives and Marketing of the Republic of Kenya.

Two-thirds of the delegates were from Kenya,
twelve came from neighboring Tanzania, eight from
Uganda, and one or two each from Zambia, Tunisia,
Nigeria, and Mauritius. Also, four representatives
of the FAO, CUNA, and Israel attended. Altogether,
there were about 100 participants from ten different
countries.

The management official of the Tunisian National

Agricultural Bank in Tunis described the government's development program in which "the problem of savings" forms an integral part, and discussed the creation of Rural Banks of Mutual Credit, which he said were "still in the experimental stage." He emphasized three elements of psychological preparation as necessary for the success of such institutions--continued education to inculcate the desire to save, clearly defining the objectives of saving according to the social habits, and creating an atmosphere of confidence.

The Parliamentary Secretary of the Ministry of Mines and Cooperatives of Zambia reported on his country's difficulties in consolidating the numerous credit and savings services provided by commercial banks, building societies, and semigovernmental agencies such as the Post Office Savings Bank and the Land and Agricultural Bank. Their "attractive rates of interest make it difficult for members of thrift cooperatives to be truly loyal," he observed. He felt that the success of the consolidation plan depended on the government's ability to create a semigovernmental organization to take over the functions of the credit cooperatives, and that only credit cooperatives could "curb the small and scattered savings of farmers, fishermen, and villagers to the benefit of economic development within the country."

The Senior Cooperative Officer of Tanzania reported on credit-union development as a part of the current Five Year Development Plan. He sought suggestions on how to eliminate prohibitive sections of the existing cooperative law. He gave some interesting background of the credit-union history in Tanzania: "Most people, especially the peasant farmers, usually prefer to keep their money, sometimes dug in the ground and elsewhere." But this has been changed "through the assistance and help of our Catholic missionaries. Of the seventy-four credit unions in Tanzania, nearly half have been sponsored by the missions and are operating near, if not within, mission premises. People, especially non-Christians, who have seen such credit unions believe that credit unions are religious associations and

therefore should be left for Christians alone."   It
was hoped that education would eliminate this mis-
apprehension.

In conclusion, the officer stated: "Credit
unions being human institutions admirably suited to
perform social as well as economic tasks . . . the
credit-union program has been initiated . . . in order to afford the average man the opportunity to ex-
hibit his responsibility, honesty, and leadership."

A credit specialist from AID assigned to assist
the development of the Cooperative Credit and Rural
Thrift Schemes in the 1,700 marketing societies of
Uganda reported on a plan recommended to the Uganda
cooperative movement by the chief officer of the
Agricultural Credit Department of the Reserve Bank
of India.   The credit plan has been operating since
1961, and was enlarged in 1964 by a Thrift Scheme.
Both plans were applied in most of the village marketing cooperatives and are based on strict rules of
credit reliability.   Repayments are made from sale
proceeds of the members' crops.   Government subsidies
are granted for the employment of able, well-educated
managers.   Sound methods are prescribed for administering deposits, which are re-lent to members through
the Credit Scheme.   In addition to the Credit and
Thrift operations performed by the marketing cooperatives, credit unions of the CUNA type are allowed to
operate, but their activities are restricted to
groups of wage and salary earners.   The success of
the credit unions--of which thirty-one with 1,800
members were registered at the end of 1964--indicated
a surprising potential for accumulating savings capital even among wage and salary earners in rural
areas of a country like Uganda if appropriate means
are employed.

Savings and credit societies were established
in Mauritius by the colonial regime around 1910 and
developed successfully, according to the report of
the island's Deputy Registrar of Cooperative Societies.   A new ordinance to constitute and control
cooperatives was promulgated in 1945, and the Mauritius Cooperative Central Bank was established in

1948, with the launching of a campaign for the formation of school savings banks to secure "deposits" to
feed the Bank. "Of the thirty-one school cooperatives, only fifteen have survived. The report attri-
butes the failures to the lack of proper education
and information facilities to spread the idea of
thrift. Of thirty-seven societies other than school
cooperatives, whose members were planters as well as
wage earners, only ten have been able to amass large
sums of deposits. In 1960, a credit union affiliated
with CUNA was established with the help of a philanthropic group. It comprises employees of private
firms and is "progressing slowly and steadily."

A more encouraging report, emphasizing the human element in cooperative credit and thrift actions,
was presented by the president of the Credit Union
League of Tanganyika. He remarked: "Having begun
in a small way, the growth of credit unions has been
quite encouraging. This has been brought about mainly by the spoken word followed by action. In Tanzania, all members of credit unions must think in terms
of individuals, individual happiness and individual
misery. How should each man be treated in view of
his happiness and his misery? The answer can never
be obtained so long as it is not clear--what man is.
This is not a matter of ideologies--an objective
truth with regard to the reality of man. Credit
unions follow, appreciate, and encourage the right
trend in recognition of the rights of man, acting for
solving problems that lower the human dignity." The
president then described the present situation as
rather encouraging, although "on the dark side is the
lack of know-how." He felt that additional education
was required.

Besides representatives of individual African
countries, a number of consultants from foreign
countries, representatives of the Catholic Church,
leaders of cooperative organizations (other than
credit unions), trade-union leaders, and educators
addressed the conference.

The members finally voted in favor of some resolutions and recommendations, prepared by five

Special Interest Committees, asking for:

1) Close ties between credit unions and other cooperative societies in all efforts toward thrift promotion.

2) Establishment of private voluntary social agencies "in order to advise the government in all matters related to cooperative credit and saving activities."

3) Mutual assistance between trade unions and cooperatives in the program of mobilizing savings among wage and salary earners.

4) The fullest use of all available manpower and institutions of training and education.

5) Establishment of cooperative banks in all countries concerned, with cooperative organizations as the major shareholders.

An appendix to the Recommendations, submitted by the Committee on Education and Training, ends with this sentence: "Care should be taken that the spirit of self-help, self-reliance, and free voluntary service be instilled in the members throughout the training."

THE FAO REGIONAL SEMINAR ON COOPERATIVE FARMING
(New Delhi, India, May, 1966)

The seminar was organized by the FAO in collaboration with the Indian Government, and convened in New Delhi during the first half of May, 1966. Eight regions were represented by a total of twenty-four delegates from India, Japan, Korea, Malaysia, Nepal, the Philippines, Thailand, and Hong Kong. The seminar was also attended by observers from AID, the U.N., the ILO, the Cooperative League of the U.S.A., the International Cooperative Alliance, and the National Cooperative Union of India. A representative of the Indian Government acted as seminar director. An FAO specialist on cooperatives was co-director. The Indian Minister of Food, Agriculture, Community

Development, and Government, Mr. C. Subramaniam, and the Deputy Minister of the same department, Mr. S. D. Misra, opened the seminar.

The Indian Minister saw cooperative farming as "a possible means of improvement" where, as in India, small, uneconomical holdings with inappropriate implements and outdated methods of cultivation hampered progress. He pointed to the inherent difficulties, noting that "the organization and development of such societies . . . involves a very high degree of leadership, cohesion and social consciousness among members" and that "complex problems of internal management and human relationships" were involved. He stressed the need "to gain adequate experience in the working of such societies" and suggested that well-planned pilot projects be set up before developing a large-scale cooperative farming system. This cautious statement set the tone of the seminar's deliberations.

The delegates, seeking a clear definition of "cooperative farming," agreed that it applied to "the forms of cooperative farming in which land, as the principal instrument of the enterprise, is pooled and managed as an integrated unit." In some regions, the term is applied loosely and includes the provision of irrigation facilities, subletting by landlords to farmers, and other methods differently classified elsewhere. Of the countries participating in the New Delhi seminar, cooperative farming societies as defined above had been organized since 1960 in India, Japan, Korea, and the Philippines.

By the end of December, 1965, about 5,000 societies had come into being in India. They had 103,000 members and covered an area of 550,000 acres. Between 1961 and 1965, 5,000 such societies were introduced in Japan. They were organized primarily for animal husbandry, fruit growing, and rice culture. In Korea, cooperative farms were organized in 1962, mostly in connection with land-reclamation proceeds. The Korean Government set up pilot farms in five districts, to which settlement or resettlement farms in five more districts were to be added. In 1965, a total of 7,200 persons (1,200 households) were living on cooperative

farms in Korea. The report adds to these rather encouraging data, resulting from the first four years
of the respective programs, that a tendency to revert
to individual cultivation was observed among the initial settlers after a few years of working cooperatively.

Not until 1965 was the organization of cooperative farms launched in the Philippines. One society
was organized in each of the islands' fifty-six provinces. Two or more societies are planned in each
province, when enough practical experience has been
gained.

The seminar considered the applicability to
Asian countries of cooperatives like those developed
in Israel and Poland, where public life is dominated
by specific ideologies. Despite the success of
cooperative-farming methods in these two countries,
the application of these methods to Asia was regarded
as unfeasible. The seminar felt that production
could be "cooperativized" in the Far East but that
the individual member should preserve his "separate
independent family life."

Special consideration was given to the matter of
membership. A basic principle of successful cooperative farming calls for "homogeneity of the members'
economic and social standing." Members should be active farmers of more or less commensurate properties.
Conflicting interests would lead to the societies'
disintegration, and different ethnic and cultural
origins would make it necessary to provide a variety
of educational, religious, and housing facilities
and thus add to the societies' overhead and compli-
cate management.

These and other considerations voiced during
the seminar show the Asian leaders' concern with the
strongly individualistic disposition of the East
Asian farm population. The Asians are unwilling to
stake all their land to a cooperative enterprise.
The practice of meeting consumption or ceremonial expenses by mortgaging the land has led to partial
pooling. But this results in the pooling of inferior

lots only, and the farmers' loyalty to the society
is divided.

It can be seen that agriculture in Asia is "not
merely a business to the farmers but a way of life,"
and breeds in the farmers a strong attachment to
their land. "Owning a small piece of land and cultivating it according to their own will provides a
great psychological satisfaction."

Later on, the discussion centered around the
criteria for judging a farming society's performance.
The report states that "the success of a cooperative
farm should not be weighed merely from the point of
view of economic achievement," and that it is also
necessary "to take into consideration the success
achieved in the social aspects." The seminar put
the "development of a spirit of cooperation among the
members" before economic achievements. A further
criterion was the degree to which "a process of social change in the villages" is initiated through a
cooperative's activities, and how its work manages
to "instill in the rural communities a proper set of
values and principles."

These are extraordinarily high criteria, and
reflect deep insight into the requirements and potentialities of cooperative work. No form of cooperation presents graver social and psychological problems than cooperative production.

In its summary, the seminar listed cautious
recommendations for the steps to be undertaken in
preparation of a cooperative farming program. The
advantages of "joint use of land, including . . .
pooling of land" are acknowledged in principle, but
the technical, social, and psychological difficulties in cooperative farming are strongly underscored.
In fact, the seminar's conclusions are more in the
character of warnings than recommendations. Their
core can be seen in one of the last paragraphs of
the report:

The spread and the success of cooperative
farming programs depend upon the extent to

which its basic idea has been accepted at
all levels of government and also the public in general. In achieving this objective, the superiority of cooperative farming should be tested through the organization of pilot projects. These pilot projects should test the comparative effectiveness of different forms of cooperative
farming, discussed in the seminar.

THE SECOND INTER-AMERICAN CONFERENCE
OF MINISTERS OF LABOR
(Carabelleda Parish, Venezuela, May, 1966)

Three years after the first conference was held
in Bogotá, Colombia, in May, 1963, the Labor Ministers of the United States and seventeen Latin American countries convened again to give special consideration to "Labor-Union Based Cooperatives," as recommended by the first conference. A study report on
"Cooperatives, Trade Unions, and Vocational Training
Institutions," issued in April, 1966, by OAS, was
among the preparatory documents presented to the
Venezuela Conference. The first conclusion of the
study report reads: "The labor and cooperative movements should combine their technical and financial
resources to create labor-cooperative human capital."

Combined training and education efforts should
be planned. The study group's basic idea was that
"by promoting cooperatives not only would these institutions have the advantage of adding new dimen-
sions to their programs but they would also provide
the workers with modern democratic means of social
and economic rehabilitation." The latter point evi-
dently reflects the group's primary interest, and an
enlargement of the cooperative program was thought
to be the appropriate instrument. The Ministers of
Labor agreed upon a large number of "recommendations
for immediate action," of which the following refer
to cooperatives:

1) Beginning in 1967, training programs for
leaders of trade-union-sponsored cooperatives shall

be inaugurated.

2) Intercooperative relations between agricultural, marketing, and consumer cooperatives shall be
established.

3) The Institute for Cooperative Development of
America, with headquarters in Peru, shall be supported by the OAS and all its member states.

4) The Program of Cooperatives of the OAS shall
be provided with sufficient resources to meet the increasing demands for cooperative assistance.

5) The various agencies providing assistance
shall give preference to the promotion of cooperatives, using joint action so far as possible for
plans requiring help from several sources.

It certainly is of great sociological significance that the Conference agreed upon the appropriate-
ness of sponsoring cooperative movements in the interest of labor. However, cooperative policies that
are one-sided in favor of organized labor and the
working classes lead to conflicts with other professional and social groups and endanger the cooperative
principle of political neutrality.

THE SEVENTH COOPERATIVE SEMINAR OF THE INTERNATIONAL
COOPERATIVE TRAINING CENTER AT THE
UNIVERSITY OF WISCONSIN
(Madison, Wisconsin, January-June, 1966)

Various reports presented to the 1963 and 1964
Cooperative Seminars of the Wisconsin Training Center
have been quoted extensively in earlier chapters.
The 1966 seminar was of special significance because
of the large number of reports presented by cooperators abroad. They show the growing recognition of
the predominance of social and human elements in cooperative developments during the past few years.

Among the motivations to promote cooperative
establishments, the following individual aspects were

emphasized:

Nigeria. The influx of farmers from rural
areas into cities must be stopped by settling or re-
settling as many of the impoverished peasants as possible. The government's industrialization program
is condemned to failure if not accompanied by adequate agricultural progress. However, farmers retained in the country with government help may get
the idea that they are government employees and mere
wage earners. To avoid this misconception, cooperative farm settlements are recommended. Special attention must be given to the moral, social, and
physical fitness of farmers to be settled cooperatively. At an early stage, the settlers are to be housed
in dormitories to give them, in the words of the report, a "we-feeling," the main prerequisites of successful cooperative work.

Zambia. Prejudices against cooperative societies, a holdover from the colonial era when natives
were excluded from European farmer cooperatives,
hamper social and educational progress in Zambia.
But cooperatives are urgently needed to guide the
people toward social activity. For this reason, the
President of Zambia promised initial governmental
loans for the establishment of cooperative bodies.
On this basis, the people of Zambia began to join
the movement. By the end of 1965, about 400 new cooperative societies were registered.

Tanzania. Efforts to mobilize the hidden savings of parts of the Tanzanian rural population led
to the recognition that mutual confidence and a sense
of responsibility can be developed only where credit-
union-like methods are taught. After appropriate
education of the prospective members, this type of
cooperative credit and savings society can be established.

Nepal. Cooperatives are expected to be the only
organizations capable of helping overcome Nepal's
two biggest obstacles to progress--the land-tenure
system and illiteracy.

Venezuela. The country's various types of co-operative institutions are characterized as still in an "embryonic state." A cooperative center and the Faculty of Economics of a leading university in Venezuela help in educating cooperative members and officers. The paramount objective of the education is "to awaken in the individual a spirit of cooperation and a completely new way of thinking, which would not be just a desire for material gains, but for mutual cooperation for the good of all people."

Cyprus. An extensive report by a Cyprus representative noted that "apart from its contribution in meeting and solving the economic problems of the rural areas, co-ops play a very important role in promoting the social and educational standards of the farmers by giving them the opportunity of taking active part in the affairs of the society." The report, one of the most optimistic presented at the 1966 seminar, was the only one discussing in detail the development of school cooperatives. The school cooperatives are a highly effective tool of cooperative education and may have contributed to the success of the Cyprus movement.

In the elementary schools of Cyprus, ninety cooperative societies were established "to create a spirit of understanding and cooperation among the members and to prepare them to become good citizens and good cooperators." The school cooperatives undertake poultry or rabbit breeding, growing of small trees or flowers, or keeping small canteens or groceries for school pupils. A committee of five pupils, elected by the pupil members, directs the societies. The teachers have advisory duties only, and cannot interfere with the cooperative work. Surpluses are used for social or philanthropic purposes, for picnics, and for buying useful equipment for the schools.

Besides these societies, there are cooperative school savings societies in every elementary and some high schools. They were introduced as early as 1950. The teachers collect the pupils' weekly savings and deposit them with the local cooperative credit society. Every pupil gets an individual

account annually, with the same interest generally
paid on fixed-term deposits. Withdrawals can be
made after the pupil has finished his schooling. At
the end of 1963, total deposits of the 433 Greek cooperative societies in Cyprus amounted to about 8.5
million pounds. Of this sum, more than 1 million
pounds, nearly 11 per cent, came from the school cooperatives. This is a remarkable accomplishment,
financially as well as educationally.

India. A special report on a cooperative experiment, the "Karpur Farm Project" in the Indian
State of Madya Pradesh, was presented to the seminar
by the project's leader, a Catholic priest. The report is significant for the sociological and psychological problems that were confronted and for how
they were solved.

Half of the Karpur district population belong
to the lowest social class, the untouchables. They
were weavers, but lost their jobs to the cloth mills.
Father Ziliak, the experiment leader, directed his
attention mainly toward this class, who suffered the
most under the extremely hard conditions in the district. The unending hardships had created a general
atmosphere of fatalism, even among the still employed
part of the population. Father Ziliak calls this
state of mind "the malady of poverty of the spirit."
He sees poverty as both an ethical and economic problem, and believes that "education in the context of
hope is the immediate step that must be taken to
satisfy the crying and immediate physical need of today," to get the people "out of this situation of
hopelessness." He found that a combination of adult
education and hard work could lead the workers "out
of their prison of ignorance and poverty." For this
purpose, the Karpur Farm was established, and has
since proved successful. Soil conservation, proper
seed preparation, plant spacing, irrigation, and the
correct choice of fertilizers and insecticides were
the result of a long period of experimentation. For
marketing purposes, the services of a nearby cooperative society were mobilized, and considerable
profits were realized.

Slowly the workers came to understand that it was really possible to increase the yield, and neighboring farmers began to apply the successfully demonstrated Karpur Farm production plan. A cooperative society was established to supply the farmers of the district with mechanized power. Tractors, a threshing machine, and transport media owned by the cooperative are hired to members and nonmembers, thus covering operating expense and depreciation. For the lighter equipment, such as irrigation pumps, which individual farmers need permanently, loans are granted by a cooperative bank in the district. Heavy equipment is loaned only to those who agree to supervision by a special cooperative committee.

The close ties between the Karpur cooperative and neighboring marketing cooperatives enable Karpur to concentrate on production and the primary objective: increasing the yield and quality of its produce. But it was hoped that a multipurpose cooperative society could be set up in the near future as a combination credit, service, and transportation unit. Following are some characteristic sentences from Father Ziliak's report:

> The organizers [of similar projects] must be thoroughly acquainted with the social and economic needs of the people. . . . Cooperatives can be used to channelize into the mainstream of the farmers' lives the moral and ethical principles that are necessary for integrity, the foundation of the new monument to be built in the hearts and minds of the people. . . . The principles of cooperation are best propagated by living them and applying them. . . . We cannot separate the economic aspects of people's lives from the ethical any more than the body and soul can be divided and still have a living person. . . . Cooperatives must move on all fronts, and not only in one sector.

THE WORLD LAND REFORM CONFERENCE
(FAO Headquarters, Rome, Italy, June-July, 1966)

The conference, sponsored by the United Nations and the FAO in association with the ILO, drew 330 participants. Twenty-six government representatives came from Africa, twenty from Asia, thirty-one from Eastern Europe, fifty-six from Latin America, twenty-nine from the Middle East, and sixty-three from North America and Western Europe. The remainder were specially invited guests of the sponsoring organizations and inter- and non-governmental bodies.

The main work of the conference was conducted in three sections: a) "Problems of Land Tenure and Structural Reform," b) "Social and Economic Aspects of Land Reform," and c) "Administrative, Financial and Training Aspects of Land Reform."

In considering structural reform, the first working group discussed cooperative-collective action in detail. Questions were raised as to whether material incentives can and should have a place in a cooperative system. The majority favored incentives and recognized the importance of non-economic incentives for agricultural development. With regard to "the role of ideology and political considerations" in organizing cooperative farms, a large number of participants felt that cooperative farming is essentially an economic and organizational arrangement, and that ideological considerations can be kept out in the initial phases.

Supporting measures such as cooperatives were held to be vital ingredients of land reform, and should be treated as such and not "as something which is an appendix to it." It was recognized that cooperatives can provide a framework for training in self-help and mutual aid. Many participants felt that only genuine cooperative societies "catering to the needs of the bulk of the peasantry and not serving the interests of the small group of rural elite can fulfill their objectives."

Cooperatives were regarded as one of the most

efficient tools in "the spreading of literacy as a
sine qua non for the success of the land-reform program"; they can and should "inculcate the spirit of
self-help and self-reliance in the communities they
service."

In its only remark on cooperatives, the second
working group stated that cooperatives can best be
organized in countries where communal obligations
have persisted, and that modern types of cooperatives
can be developed "if due care is taken to link these
modern institutions with existing values and outlooks."

The third working section of the conference,
which was primarily concerned with the over-all aspects of land reform, concluded that a basic requirement for land-reform programs was suitable arrangements for "supporting services for reform, such as
credit, extension and cooperatives."

A similar remark is contained in the summary
report by the general rapporteur, J. A. C. Davies,
the Chief Agricultural Officer of the Sierre Leona
Ministry of Natural Resources. He observes that "this
Conference has clearly stated that no land-reform
program can succeed if not supported by credit, cooperatives, education, and training services, and only
where all these measures are phased and coordinated
in the proper way will land reform be a success."

The first recommendation of the final conference
resolution asks the United Nations and the FAO to
continue "to provide the necessary assistance . . .
for the planning and implementation of land-reform
measures, including supporting services." This is a
request for supporting cooperatives where they are
part of the respective programs.

THE FIRST INTERNATIONAL CONFERENCE ON COOPERATIVE
ASSISTANCE TO DEVELOPING COUNTRIES
(Fredensborg, Denmark, September, 1965)

The conference brought together for the first
time international cooperative organizations,

representatives of national cooperative movements, and officials of governmental agencies with interests and responsibilities in cooperative forms of development and aid to developing nations. Governments of eight Western countries and Israel, cooperative organizations of nine Western countries and Poland, and four international organizations (FAO, ILO, ICA, OECD) were represented among the twenty-five official participants.

More than a year before the Fredensborg Conference, the first paragraph of the last chapter of this book, "Coordinating Aid to Cooperative Movements in Developing Countries," was written and forwarded as a separate memorandum to some interested organizations in the United States. This action, the result of personal contacts, was evidence of common concern over the lack of the international coordination required for effective cooperative work abroad. It is, therefore, of great satisfaction to this writer that the subject of the conference and its "Recommendations for Action" reflect the author's identical concern: the urgent need to improve international coordination and information techniques.

The conferences dealt exclusively with the problem of avoiding duplication and waste in the efforts of the participants to aid the cooperative movement in countries. Thus, the internal aspects of cooperative work in individual countries, such as the particular social and human conditions, were not the topic of discussion. Still, the importance of the conference as the first international meeting of this kind makes it imperative to review it briefly, even though it did not directly contribute to the content of this book.

Ways to exchange information on means of cooperative aid to developing countries were discussed. It was unanimously agreed that an international agency was required to channel information to all interested organizations. The International Cooperative Alliance offered to publish, before the end of 1965, a Calendar of Events for 1966, covering seminars and other important events in the international cooperative field. Basic data were expected to be furnished to the ICA by nongovernment agencies of the member countries and by the FAO and ILO. It was proposed that use be made of the Development Assistance Committee of the OECD in Paris. An OECD representative said that cooperative work was going to be included in the program of his organization which, until recently, had not been directly involved in cooperatives.

The conference also decided to promote the preparation of an inventory of current cooperative research projects, and to help in the compilation of a glossary of technical terms used in cooperative work, in English, French, Spanish, and German. Guidelines were set for the improvement of cooperative seminars and other training institutions proposed by the discussion groups.

The recruitment and practical work of experts either to be sent abroad or to lead training courses in Western countries was widely discussed. Here the individual and non-economic factors of cooperative aid came to the foreground. The conference report states:

"It has been clearly shown that expert orientation prior to going overseas reduces the number of failures and misfits by providing a greater understanding of living conditions, social, cultural, and religious factors, etc."

The significance of the Fredensborg Conference as a first official step toward international coordination can hardly be overstated. Much, of course, depends on the follow-up to the conference work, which could not be expected to be more than a tentative approach to problems that are highly complicated and global in extent. It is to be hoped that the ICA and OECD offers to serve as centers of information will be effectively supported by governments and private agencies. International coordination should be an ongoing undertaking, functioning systematically in the interests of everyone involved in cooperative aid, instead of remaining a topic at international meetings. It is encouraging that the

Fredensborg Conference emphasized these points and decided to follow up the work already begun in a second conference to convene in a year or two.

THE FIRST INTERNATIONAL CONFERENCE OF THE MAJOR COOPERATIVE THRIFT AND CREDIT ORGANIZATIONS
(Jamaica, October, 1966)

At the invitation of CUNA International, more than 100 delegates representing sixty organizations in thirty countries assembled for a five-day conference in Jamaica. Its objective was to exchange views on present and future aims of cooperative thrift and credit organizations. Although the program was not directed toward cooperative activities in developing countries, numerous topics belonged to this field. The most important decision made in this connection was to establish a continuing committee under the joint responsibility of CUNA International and the ICA. The committee was to coordinate future activities of the participants and study certain suggestions made during the conference. In the words of the conference report, the committee's work "included study of possible plans for international lending that would facilitate a flow of needed funds from wealthier movements to those in emerging or developing areas, . . . a system of guarantee or insurance . . . for such interlending system, . . . establishment of an international educational and training system."[1] Prominent representatives of different organizations emphasized the priority of these plans at the closing session assembled to evaluate the conference performance. Among them were Pierre Latour, president of the Caisse Central de Crédit Coopératif, France, and Hector Zayas-Chardon, director of the Inter-American Cooperative Finance Development Society, Washington, D.C.

The elected permanent chairman of the conference, A. R. Glen, of British Columbia, president of CUNA International, pointed to "the human, people-to-people aspects of the credit union and cooperative movement," stressing the basic principle that must dominate all cooperative work.

NOTE TO CHAPTER 6

1. Credit Union Magazine (the official publication of CUNA International) (December, 1966).

CHAPTER 7 COORDINATING AID TO
COOPERATIVE MOVEMENTS
IN DEVELOPING COUNTRIES

A duplication of efforts, sometimes even conflicting programs initiated by national and international agencies engaged in cooperative work in developing countries, has in recent years repeatedly jeopardized the effectiveness of such aid, wasted human and material resources, and even undermined the position of foreign advisers in the eyes of governments and people receiving assistance from Western organizations. Instances of such disturbances, which the author himself has encountered during his work, have been cited by representatives of most American and European agencies, with whom he has been in contact. They have often bitterly complained of the lack of coordination among the organizations involved. Reference to this problem has been made in the FAO report on financing agricultural developments in Asian and African countries, outlined in the earlier chapter on "Cooperative Credit and Savings."

Such inconsistencies and uncoordinated initiatives are particularly dangerous to the essential elements of building cooperative movements, which embrace the individual and social conditions of their constituents as well their economic interests. Because of the widespread application of cooperative methods for the most urgent tasks in developing countries, i.e., agricultural reforms as the main basis of economic and social improvements, the support of cooperative movements appears to be a universal factor in development policies. Only if this support is unhampered by conflicting plans and ideas can it lead to more dramatic improvements in social and individual conditions than may be accomplished

by larger industrial projects and more comprehensive
programs of technical assistance.

The inconveniences characterized above are the
residue of the truly chaotic beginning of help to
newly developing communities in the early 1950's.
However, the remaining disturbances are less significant than were anticipated under the circumstances
described in the following paragraphs. But this encouraging factor does not lessen the need for drastic
efforts to improve the still defective coordination.

The many-sided actions to aid the building of
cooperative movements, and the far-reaching and
numerous public and private initiatives to this end,
started and continued under the pressure of worldwide disorders. As never before, whole continents
seemed to burst with long-withheld energies, all directed toward unlimited expectations, and all deprived of the means to achieve them. Over the few
decades since the beginning of this explosive movement, political and social crises in even the most
stable countries prevented adequate preparations to
meet the extensive and unforseeable requirements of
an effective policy to promote development. In addition, the cold war injected political implications
into the essentially neutral and peaceful aim of
aiding poor nations. Politics, rather than economic
and social considerations, was often the deciding
factor in the allocation of subsidies. Each side
of the divided world tried to gain a political advantage over the other by being first to help the
newly emerging nations.

There was good reason for quick intervention
where cooperatives were involved. Both West and East
claim superiority for their cooperative concepts and
methods, and once one of these was applied political
consequences would soon follow. Because of this
rivalry in aid to cooperatives in developing countries,
some non-aligned governments saw an opportunity to
take advantage of their potential benefactors.

Many of the difficulties experienced in developing countries and in international negotiations arose

from these conditions. Private initiative, such as
the first spontaneous actions of cooperative associations in some Western countries, often met with resistance or reluctance from their own governments
when government help was required to supplement private funds and the projects were politically objectionable. Some coordination of private and public
action was finally accomplished in individual countries, but often too late to avoid discrepancies
caused by earlier uncontrolled actions.

Much more difficult, of course, was the avoid-
ance of uncoordinated actions on the international
level. The following examples may be cited:

a) A leading British authority on cooperation
complained about Israeli advisers to cooperatives in
an African country, charging that they taught cooperative methods contrary to traditional British concepts. He proposed appropriate steps through diplomatic channels to replace the Israeli experts with
British advisers.

b) A European agricultural organization planned
to establish cooperative schools in a developing
country, where such institutions already had been
created by an equally authorized association of another nation. The request to transfer the project
elsewhere was answered by saying that the proposed
school system would be superior and that the existing institutions would close if faced with competition.

c) Representatives of a foreign-aid team in a
Middle Eastern country tried to persuade the government to abandon certain advanced projects sponsored
by others. They promised to grant help on a larger
scale if the projects in progress were cancelled.

While good intentions may sometimes lead to
this kind of controversy, more often national, political, or personal ambitions are involved. New instruments of planning and coordination are needed
to remedy these conditions.

Within most Western countries, there are coordinating agencies already at work or in preparation. In Germany, the Free Committee of Cooperative Associations (Freier Ausschuss der Genossenschaftsverbaende) is the medium through which the four independent German associations of different types of cooperatives try to coordinate their aid programs. The Scandinavian countries and Holland each have centers directing their corresponding activities. The consumer cooperative movement in Switzerland is leading its country's aid to cooperatives abroad. The British and French organizations seem to be less unified, because of the large number of institutions with varying traditions and goals.

In the United States, the Cooperative Advisory Committee of AID is in charge of setting the basic policies of aid to cooperative movements all over the world. The Committee's first report stressed the need not only of close internal contacts but also of internal communications. The report refers to the ILO, FAO, OECD, and other international agencies with which close relations have been recently established.

The international agencies made considerable efforts to coordinate their work where common goals were pursued. The FAO has arranged regional conferences jointly sponsored by ILO and various regional bodies. They began in India in 1949, and later were held in Ceylon, Egypt, Puerto Rico, and other places. FAO and ILO have semiannual meetings geared to their common interest in developing agricultural cooperatives; they jointly sponsor cooperative courses and seminars, and arrange special conferences on technical matters and related projects. The ICA regularly invites the FAO to its biannual conferences, and an agreement has been reached regarding participation in the conduct of international cooperative schools.

The International Federation of Agricultural Producers (IFAP) has an office in Rome in order to maintain permanent contact with the FAO, and FAO representatives are permanently stationed in the regional offices of UNESCO in Cairo and Mexico. Their

primary job is to follow up cooperative movements in
these areas.

Despite all these efforts, however, until recently the results do not seem to sufficiently guarantee the required coordination. A recently published
FAO report emphasizes the damage caused by the variety of methods applied to finance agrarian reforms
in developing countries, mainly where cooperative
organizations are involved. A group of experts reported in July, 1964, after several months of study
tours in more than ten African and Asian states, that
the progress of agricultural programs is hampered by
the lack of financial coordination. Closer ties between all interested organizations are asked for in
the concluding paragraph of the FAO report. Instead
of adding more money to uncontrollable funds, all
efforts should be concentrated on improving the
structure, the methods of credit operation and of related educational institutions. This is the final
recommendation of the FAO expert group after extended
studies performed in many developing countries. It
proposes an absolutely coordinated program for reorganizing the ways and means of financing agricultural aid programs and the operations of credit cooperatives as their essential tools.

At this point, the author would like to present
the following concept of coordinating machinery,
which may be useful as a first step toward closer cooperation between contributors to cooperative movements in developing countries.

A system of a compulsory mutual exchange of information should be organized, operating without regard to the individual interests of nations, organizations, agencies, or persons. Each country would
designate a national center of information to which
all private and public organizations involved in cooperative work would be required to report all actions
of major importance planned for the near future.
This would be especially important for countries that
have received no aid from the reporting organizations.
The reports collected in the national centers would
then be forwarded to an international center of

information at regular intervals. Such an international center could be chosen, by mutual agreement
of all bodies involved, from among the existing neutral agencies of international standing: the FAO,
the ILO, the OECD, and others. The center's function
would be to register all information received according to the sources, the objectives, and the types of
the projects in preparation, and to establish contacts between organizations with common and/or conflicting interests. The international center should
issue a monthly or quarterly publication reporting
on all new actions of importance as well as on the
programs and locations of forthcoming international
and regional conferences of interest to cooperators.

     The plan must be compulsory on the national as
well as international level. Without compulsion,
the objective--complete coordination--cannot be attained. The same "cooperative discipline" that dom-
inates cooperative work should also dominate the
coordination plan. Then a way might be found to apply genuine cooperative methods, without any wasted
efforts, on the highest level to promote the great
task of building cooperative movements and furthering
projects already initiated in developing countries.

SELECTED BIBLIOGRAPHY

SELECTED BIBLIOGRAPHY

Public Documents

Agency for International Development (AID)

AID Assistance to Cooperative Enterprises, Annual
    Reports to Congress. Washington, D.C.: Fiscal
    years 1963, 1964, 1965.

Capital Formation for Development of Cooperatives.
    Washington, D.C.: 1964.

Cooperatives Democratic Institutions for Economic and
    Social Development. Washington, D.C.: 1961.

Food and Agriculture Organization of the
United Nations (FAO)

Agricultural Credit in Economically Underdeveloped
    Countries (H. Belshaw). Rome, Italy: 1959.

Cooperation in Agricultural Production (N. J. Newiger).
    Rome, Italy: 1966.

Guide to Methods and Procedures of Rural Credit
    Systems (T. S. Rao). Rome, Italy: 1962.

Report on the Development Center on Agricultural Credit
    for Africa (N. J. Newiger). Rome, Italy: 1963.

Report of the FAO Regional Seminar on Cooperative
    Farming, New Delhi, India. Rome, Italy: 1966.

Work of FAO to Assist Development of Cooperatives
    (R. H. Gretton). Rome, Italy: 1963.

219

International Labour Office (ILO)

Developments and Trends in the World Cooperative
    Movement. Geneva, Switzerland: 1962.

The Economic and Social Significance of Rural Co-
    operation (H. K. Noock). Geneva, Switzerland:
    1963.

The ILO's Operational Activities for the Promotion
    and Development of Cooperation, Rural and
    Related Institutions. Geneva, Switzerland: 1966.

Recommendation Concerning the Role of Cooperatives in
    the Economic and Social Development of Develop-
    ing Countries. Authentic text of the "Recommen-
    dation 127" adopted by the International Labour
    Conference. Geneva, Switzerland: 1966.

The Role of Cooperatives in the Economic and Social
    Development of Developing Countries. Reports
    IV (1) and (2) and VII (1) and (2). Geneva,
    Switzerland: 1964, 1965, 1966.

Organization of American States (OAS)

The Agricultural Cooperative Movement in Latin America
    (F. Chaves). Washington, D.C.: 1962.

Cooperative America. Washington, D.C.: 1962.

Progress-Problems-Potentials of Latin American Coops
    (F. Chaves). Washington, D.C.: 1961.

Report on the First Meeting of the Inter-American
    Committee on the Alliance of Progress.
    Washington, D.C.: 1964.

Reports on the Second Inter-American Conference of
    Ministers of Labor on the Alliance of Progress
    in Venezuela. Washington, D.C.: 1966.

Reports

The Cooperative League of the U.S.A.

Cooperative League Work in Latin America, East Paki-
    stan, Malawi, Vietnam. Chicago, Ill.: 1964.

Cooperatives--Hope of the World. Chicago, Ill.: 1964.

Cooperatives Offer Emerging Nations a Private Way
    (J. Voorhis). Chicago, Ill.: 1962.

Reports from Danish Conference on International
    Cooperative Assistance. Chicago, Ill.: 1965.

Socio-Economic Development of Cooperatives in
    Latin America. Chicago, Ill.: 1963.

CUNA International (formerly: Credit
Union National Association)

Annual Report CUNA World Extension Department.
    Madison, Wisconsin: 1966.

CUNA/AID Program. Madison, Wisconsin: 1966.

CUNA Progress Report Latin America. Madison,
    Wisconsin: 1966.

Investors in the Future (Progress Report). Madison,
    Wisconsin: 1967.

Report on the Development of the Pilot Project in
    Carachi-Ecuador. Madison, Wisconsin: 1965.

Report on the Fourth African Conference on Mobiliza-
    tion of Savings. Madison, Wisconsin: 1965.

National Farmers Union

Bench Marks of Farmers Union. Washington, D.C.: 1963.

The Fifth Far East Agricultural Credit and Coopera-
    tive Workshop. Washington, D.C.: 1965.

NFU/AID Cooperative Development Program (John M.
    Eklund). Washington, D.C.: 1963.

Partners in Development Around the World. Washington,
    D.C.: 1964.

                    Other Sources

Deutscher Raiffeisenwerband (German Association of
    Rural Cooperatives). The Greek Agricultural
    Cooperative Movement and the Panhellenic Confed-
    eration of Unions of Agricultural Cooperatives.
    Bonn, Germany: 1960.

Economic Research Institute (IFO). Cooperative
    Farming in Kenya and Tanzania (N. J. Newiger).
    Munich, Germany: 1967.

Friedrich Ebert-Foundation. The Cooperative Movement
    in Egypt. Bonn, Germany: 1962.

German Foundation for Developing Countries, Seminar
    Reports. Berlin-Tegel, Germany: 1960, 1962.

Insurance Committee of the International Cooperative
    Alliance. Cooperative Insurance Establishments
    in Developing Countries. Washington, D.C.:
    Cooperative League of the U.S.A., 1963.

The International Cooperative Training Center. Hand-
    books of Cooperative Seminars. Madison,
    Wisconsin: 1963, 1964, 1966.

International Federation of Agricultural Credit.
    Problems of Credit Development in Africa.
    Paris, France: 1965.

Plunkett Foundation for Cooperative Studies. Annual
    Reports of the Plunkett Foundation for Coopera-
    tive Studies. London, England: 1962-65.

United Nations 39th Session, Fourth Report. <u>Progress of Agricultural Reforms</u>. New York, 1965.

Waidelich, W. <u>Report on a Study Tour to Nigeria</u>. Stuttgart-Hohenheim, Germany: Cooperative School, 1963.

Periodicals

<u>Credit Union Magazine</u>. Madison, Wisconsin: CUNA International, March, 1962--February, 1968.

<u>Finance and Development</u>. Vol. 3/4. Washington, D.C.: The International Monetary Fund and the International Bank for Reconstruction and Development, 1966/1967.

<u>International Cooperative Training Journal</u>. Vol. 1/2. Madison, Wisconsin: The International Cooperative Training Center, 1965, 1966.

<u>Land Reform</u>. Rome, Italy: Food and Agriculture Organization of the United Nations (FAO), 1963-67.

<u>News for Farmer Cooperatives</u>. Washington, D.C.: U.S. Department of Agriculture, March, 1958--August, 1967.

Books

<u>The Cooperative as a Development Tool</u>. Joint publication of the Cooperative League of the U.S.A., CUNA International, Farmers Union International Assistance Corp., Foundation for Cooperative Housing, International Cooperative Development Association, International Cooperative Training Center, Washington, D.C., 1966.

Croteau, John T. <u>The Economics of the Credit Union</u>. Detroit, Michigan: Wayne State University Press, 1963.

Digby, Margaret. <u>A World Look at Coops</u>. London, England: The Plunkett Foundation for Cooperative Studies, 1960.

Mulick, M. A. H. Assessment of Economic Planning in Pakistan. Bonn, Germany, 1960.

Myrdal, Gunnar. Asian Drama, an Inquiry into the Poverty of Nations. New York: Pantheon Books, Inc., 1968.

Tinbergen, Jan. Design of Development. Baltimore, Maryland: The Johns Hopkins Press, 1958.

Waterton, A. Development Planning. The Economic Development Institute--International Bank for Reconstruction and Development. Baltimore, Maryland: The Johns Hopkins Press, 1965.

INDEX

AARRO (see Afro-Asian
  Rural Reconstruc-
  tion Organization)
Abrahamsen, Martin A.,
  70, 100, 156
Afghanistan, 162
Africa, 124-25 (see also
  individual countries)
African Conference on
  the Mobilization of
  Local Savings
  (Nairobi, 1965),
  190-94
Afro-Asian Rural Recon-
  struction Organiza-
  tion (AARRO), 34, 171
Agency for International
  Development (AID), 27,
  30, 60, 108, 111, 113-
  14, 118, 128, 156,
  171, 174, 192, 194,
  213
Agrarian reform, 169; in
  Egypt, 36-41
Agrarian Reform Coopera-
  tive Department (Egypt),
  40
Agricultural and Coop-
  erative Credit Bank
  (Agricultural Bank
  of Egypt), 94-95,
  96, 140
Agricultural coopera-
  tives, 175-76
in Pakistan, 68-69
Agricultural credit,
  88, 130, 181, 189

Agriculture, U.S. Depart-
  ment of, 70, 100-101,
  115
AID (see Agency for Inter-
  national Development)
Algeria, 7, 125, 127
All India Cooperative
  Union, 143
Alliance for Progress,
  108, 128
Anderson, Lyle, 149-51
"Antigonish Movement"
  (Canada), 158
Arab States Training
  Center for Education
  for Community Develop-
  ments, 142
Argentina, 63, 157
Asia, 125-26 (see also
  individual countries)
Ataturk (Mustapha Kemal),
  17, 18
Avram, Percy, 117$\underline{n}$.

Bailey, A. A., 161
Banda, H. K., 149
Bank of Agriculture (Iran),
  143
Basutoland, 121
Bernstein, Joel, 172
Betshuana, 121
Bolivia, 59
Brazil, 51, 63, 156, 157
British Cooperative Col-
  lege (London), 158

Burma, 7, 135
  consumer cooperatives
    in, 61
  credit and savings
    policies in, 106–107
  and foreign influence,
    14–15

Caisse Central de Crédit
  Coopératif (France), 208
Cambodia, 30–31
Cameroun, 57–58, 61, 144
Canada, 158
Capital mobilization, 172
Center Nacional de la
  Cooperation Agricole
  (Paris), 144
Central African Republic,
  119, 144–45
Central Association of
  Cooperative Unions
  (Greece), 92–93
Central Bank for Coop-
  eratives (Peru), 115
Central Bank of the
  Philippines, 179–80
Central Committee for
  Cooperative Education
  (India), 143, 144
Central Cooperative
  Society (Jordan), 126
Central Organization of
  Agricultural Coopera-
  tives (Egypt), 140
Central Organization of
  Industrial Cooperatives
  (Egypt), 55
Centralized credit, 92
Ceylon, 74, 84, 129, 213
  consumer cooperatives
    in, 61
Chaves, F., 51–52, 63,
  156

Children (see School
  cooperatives)
Chile, 63
Collective farming, 67,
  69–72
  discouraging results of,
    76–78
  in Poland, 80–83 (see
    also Agricultural
    cooperatives)
Collectivism (see Coopera-
  tive Collective Produc-
  tion)
Collège Coopératif (Paris),
  158
College for Economic and
  Cooperative Science
  (Thailand), 126
Colombia, 60, 126–27, 128
Colonialism, 4–5, 16, 168,
  188
Comilla experiment (East
  Pakistan), 152–54
Congo, 12, 125, 127, 188
Consumer cooperatives,
  60–63, 156, 167
  failure of, 63
Cooperation, defined, 23
Cooperative Advisory Com-
  mittee (AID), 213
Cooperative Central Bank
  (Iraq), 125
Cooperative Central Bank
  (Thailand), 105
Cooperative-collective
  production, 66–85
Cooperative credit:
  institutions of, 130–31
  and savings, 86–137
  systems of, 93, 99–102
Cooperative education,
  138–62
Cooperative establishments,
  motivations, goals and
    obstacles for, 22–65

Cooperative farming, 74
  in Philippines, 196
  recommendations for,
    197-98
Cooperative Farming Work-
  shop (Pakistan), 73-74
Cooperative General Insur-
  ance Society (India),
  134-35
Cooperative housing pro-
  grams, 63-65
Cooperative insurance,
  133-36
Cooperative Insurance Co.
  (England), 136
Cooperative League of the
  United States, 100, 149,
  154, 171, 194
Cooperative movements,
  aid to in developing
  countries, 210-15
Cooperative Seminar
  (Iran), 143
Cooperative Seminar of the
  International Coopera-
  tive Training Center
  at the University of
  Wisconsin (Madison,
  1966), 199-205
Cooperative Societies Act
  (India, 1960), 182
Cooperative thrift and
  credit societies, 167
Cooperative village set-
  tlement projects, 77
Cooperatives:
  agricultural, 68-69,
    175-76
  consumer, 60-63, 156,
    167
  credit, 187-90, 191
  harbor workers', 83-84
  industrial, 55-58, 61
  in Israel, 196
  multipurpose, 95, 182

  in Poland, 196
  school, 48-51, 201
  trade union sponsored,
    198
  village, 171
  women's, 53-54
  workmens', 46-48, 167
Cooperatives, Credit and
  Rural Sociology Branch
  (of FAO), 35
Credit, agricultural, 88,
  130
  personal, 188
  public, in Egypt, 29
  utilization of, 129-30
Credit cooperatives, 187-
  90, 191
  and savings, 86-137
Credit delinquency, 171,
  180-81
Credit unions, 118-19, 192
Credit Union League of
  Tanganyika, 193
Credit Union Magazine
  (publ. by CUNA), 156
Credit Union National
  Association (CUNA), 31-
  32, 109, 111, 113-17,
  128, 134, 156, 174,
  190, 208
Crop rotation, 37
CUNA (see Credit Union
  National Association)
Cyprus, 61, 201
  school cooperatives in,
    50-51

Dahomey, 11, 12
Davies, J. A. C., 205
Deutcher Raiffeisenverband
  (German Central Associa-
  tion of Rural Coopera-
  tives), 162

Developing nations:
  agrarian character of,
    13-14
  aid to cooperative move-
    ments in, 210-15
  cooperative aid to, 163-
    209
  exports and imports of,
    13-14
  leaders of, 2, 3
  politico-historical and
    socio-economic factors
    in, 1-21
  religious practices in,
    2, 13
  state socialism in, 24-
    25
Directorate of Coopera-
  tives (Vietnam), 176

East Pakistan:
  Comilla experiment in,
    152-54
  studies of means of
    cooperation in, 109-10
  cooperatives in, and
    government leadership,
    30-31
  (see also Pakistan)
Economic Commission for
  Asia and the Far East
  (U.N.), 171
Ecuador, 60
Education:
  cooperative, 138-62
  and training, 172
Egypt, 8, 28, 20, 44-46,
  135, 142, 213
  Agrarian Reform Coop-
    erative Department,
    40
  agrarian reform in,
    36-41

  Agricultural Bank of,
    94-95, 96, 140
  Central Organization of
    Agricultural Coopera-
    tives, 140
  Central Organization of
    Industrial Cooperatives,
    55
  consumer cooperatives
    in, 61-62
  cotton exports of, 96-97
  feudalism in, 17-19
  harbor workers' coop-
    eratives in, 83-84
  industrial cooperatives
    in, 55-58
  land-reform cooperatives,
    93-94
  Nawag experiment in, 36-
    41
  public credit in, 29
  school cooperatives in,
    48-51
Egyptian Land Reform Law
  (1952), 93
Egyptian State Bank of
  Agriculture, 90, 94
Eklund, John M., 30-31,
  34, 100, 154, 171, 172
El Mahallah experiment
  (Egypt), 50
El Shams University
  (Cairo), 140
Ellman, A. O., 78-79
Ethiopia, 6, 112, 121
Exploitation, 8-9, 12-13
  and feudalism, 16-18
Exports, of developing
  countries, 13-14

FAO (see Food and Agri-
  cultural Organization)

FAO Regional Seminar on
   Cooperative Farming
   (New Delhi, 1966),
   194-98
Far East Agricultural
   Credit and Coopera-
   tive Workshop (Seoul,
   1965), 170-87
Farmer Cooperative Ser-
   vice (of U.S. Dept. of
   Agriculture), 70,
   100-101, 115
Farming, collective (see
   Agricultural coopera-
   tives; Collective
   farming)
Fathy, Hassan, 64
Fawzy, Mahmud, 23, 36
Feminism, 52
Feudalism:
   in Egypt, 17-19
   and exploitation,
   16-18
   in Iran, 19
Fiji Islands, 116
Food and Agricultural
   Organization (of U.N.)
   (FAO), 34, 71-72,
   120, 128-29, 142, 160,
   166, 171, 190, 194,
   204, 206, 207, 213,
   214, 215
Food for Peace, 114
Formosa, 170, 184-85
France, 144, 158, 208
Free Committee of Coop-
   erative Associations
   (Freier Ausschuss
   der Genossenschafts-
   verbaende), 160, 161,
   213
Free Trade, 13
Freier Ausschuss der
   Genossenschaftsver-
   baende (Free Committee

of Cooperative Asso-
   ciations), 160, 161,
   213
Friedrich Ebert Foundation
   (Bonn), 41

Gabon, 187
Gambia, 121
German Central Association
   of Rural Cooperatives
   (Deutcher Raiffeisenverband), 162
German Foundation for De-
   veloping Countries, 14,
   67, 143
German Rural Cooperatives,
   145
Ghana, 121, 188
Ghana:
   National Cooperative
   Insurance Company of,
   136
Glen, A. R., 208
Greece, 30, 42, 135
   Central Association of
   Cooperative Unions of,
   92-93
   cooperative movement of,
   145
   peasant farmers in, 59
   political upheavals in,
   14
   school cooperatives in,
   50-51
   State Cooperative School
   of, 145
   worker cooperation in,
   47
Greek Agricultural Bank,
   90-93
Gretton, Ronald H., 34
"Group joint liability,"
   181

Guide to Methods and Procedures of Rural Credit Surveys (publ. by FAO), 128-29

Guinea, 11, 47, 53

Harbor workers' cooperatives (Egypt), 83-84

Hirschfeld, A., 43

Home industries, 48

Honduras, 157

Hong Kong, 194

Hussain, A. F. A., 152-53

Hutchinson, C. H., 148

ICA (see International Cooperative Alliance)

IFAP (International Federation of Agricultural Producers), 34, 160, 166, 213

ILO (see International Labor Office)

Imports, of developing countries, 13-14

India, 9, 23, 30, 74, 84, 90, 145, 159, 182, 213
  All India Cooperative Union of, 143
  Central Committee for Cooperative Education, 143, 144
  collective farming in, 70, 195
  cooperative credit system of, 99-102
  Cooperative General Insurance Society of, 134-35
  cooperative programs in, 25
  Cooperative Societies Act (1960), 182
  culture of, 6
  Karpur Project in, 202
  National Cooperative Union of, 194
  native traders in, 15-16
  Production Center Cooperatives in, 101
  self-help programs in, 33-34
  State Reserve Bank of, 99, 102, 144
  women's cooperative societies in, 54

Indonesia, 4, 108
  People's Bank of, 107

Industrial cooperatives, 55-58, 59

Institute for Cooperative Credit (Iran), 143

Institute for Cooperative Development of America, 199

Insurance, cooperative, 133-36

Inter-American Conference of Ministers of Labor Carabelleda Parish, 1966), 198-99

Inter-American Cooperative Finance Development Society, 208

Inter-American Development Bank, 115

International Confederation of Agricultural Credit (Tunis, 1965), 187-94

International Conference of the Major Cooperative Thrift and Credit Organizations (Jamaica, 1966), 208

International Conference
  on Cooperative Assis-
  tance to Developing
  Countries (Denmark,
  1965), 205-8
International Cooperative
  Alliance (ICA), 22, 34,
  73-74, 129, 134, 160,
  166, 171, 206, 207, 213
International Cooperative
  Development Service (of
  U.S. Agency for Inter-
  national Development),
  159-60
International Cooperative
  Seminar (of German
  Foundation for the
  Developing Countries),
  13-14
International Federation
  of Agricultural Pro-
  ducers (IFAP), 34, 160,
  166, 213
International Labor Con-
  ferences (Geneva, 1965,
  1966), 164-70
International Labor Office
  (ILO), 43, 66-67, 83-84,
  102-4, 108, 142, 160,
  164-70, 194, 204, 206,
  207, 213, 215
International Monetary
  Fund, 175
Iran, 28, 145
  Bank of Agriculture of,
  143
  Cooperative Seminar, 143
  feudalism in, 19
  land-distribution in, 93
  nomadism in, 19
  women's cooperative
  societies in, 54
Iraq, 128, 129
  Cooperative Central
  Bank of, 125

Israel, 84, 190, 206
  cooperatives in, 196
Ivory Coast, 11, 35, 119,
  129
  National Bank of Agri-
  cultural Credit of,
  187, 188

Japan, 170, 181, 183, 194,
  195
  economic progress, and
  agricultural sector in,
  174-76
  land resources in, 185
  mutual relief associa-
  tions in, 182
  rural savings programs
  in, 184
Jordan, 128, 135
  Central Cooperative
  Society of, 126

Karpur Project (India),
  202
Kenya, 6, 121, 128, 190
  collective farming in,
  77-78
  cooperatives in, 124
  land redistribution in,
  75-76
Kim, Hak Yul, 173
Korea (see South Korea)

Land:
  consolidations of, 37
  distribution of, 93
  reform, 93-94, 204-5
  resources, 172, 185-86
  splitting, 37

Land Reform (publ. by
    FAO), 35n., 72
Latin America, 84, 126-
    27, 155-56, 157
    consumer cooperatives
    in, 61-63
    school cooperatives in,
    50-51
    (see also individual
    countries)
Latin American Credit
    Union League, 133
Latour, Pierre, 208
"Liberation Province"
    (Egypt), 8
Libya, 129, 187
Lipski, W., 80, 82-83
Loughborough Cooperative
    College (Great
    Britain), 154

McLellan, Father, 115-16
Malawi (Nyasaland), 146,
    149
Malaya, 74, 129, 135,
    136
Malaya Cooperative Insur-
    ance Society, 135
Malaysia, 194
Mali, 11
Mau Mau revolts (1963),
    75
Mauritius, 190, 192
Mauritius Cooperative
    Central Bank, 192-93
Mexico, 63
Misr Spinning and Weaving
    Company (Egypt), 48
Misra, S. D., 198
Modern Village, 80
Morocco, 187, 188
Multipurpose coopera-
    tives, 95, 182

Mustapha Kemal (Ataturk),
    17, 18
Mutual Societies of Rural
    Production (Sociétés
    Mutuelles de Production
    Rurale), 12

Nasser, Gamal Abdel, 18
National Agricultural
    Credit Office (South
    Vietnam), 176
National Bank of Agricul-
    tural Credit (Ivory
    Coast), 187, 188
National Bank of Tunisia,
    187
National Cooperative In-
    surance Company (Ghana),
    136
National Cooperative
    Marketing Association
    (New Delhi), 31
National Cooperative Union
    of India, 194
National Farmers Union
    (U.S.), 30
Nationalism, 5-6, 7
Nawag experiment (Egypt),
    36-41
Nepal, 126, 128, 194, 200
Newiger, N. J., 75-78
News for Farmer Coopera-
    tives (publ. by FCS),
    115, 156
Nicaragua, 60
Niger, 151
    cooperation in, and
    education, 26, 144
    nomads in, 26-27
    Sociétés de Prévoyance
    in, 10-11, 12
Nigeria, 121, 122, 159,
    190

colonialism in, 9, 111
cooperative schools in,
  151-52
credit cooperatives in,
  112-13
fatalism in, 42
industrial cooperatives
  in, 58-59
marketing cooperatives
  in, 53
problems of cooperative
  developments in, 200
Njassa, 121
Nomads, 6, 19, 26-27
Nook, H. K., 70-71
Nyasaland (Malawi), 146,
  149

OAS (Organization of
  American States), 51,
  63, 198, 199
OECD (Organization for
  Economic Cooperation
  and Development), 160,
  206, 207, 213, 215
Organization for Economic
  Cooperation and Develop-
  ment (OECD), 160, 206,
  207, 213, 215
Organization of American
  States (OAS), 51, 63,
  198, 199
Organization of the
  Cooperatives of
  America, 157

Pakistan, 135
  Cooperative Farming
  Workshop in, 73-74
  (see also East Paki-
  stan; West Pakistan)

Pakistani Academy for
  Rural Development, 153
Pan American Union, 128,
  155
  (see also Organization
  of American States)
Panhellenic Confederation
  of Agricultural Coop-
  eratives, 14, 145
Peace Corps, 32, 114
Peoples' Bank of Indonesia,
  107
Pernambuco, 51
Peru, 114
  Central Bank for Coop-
  eratives, 115
Peru Credit Union League,
  115
Philippine Cooperative
  Credit Union League, 174
Philippine National Coop-
  erative Bank, 174
Philippines, 170, 185,
  194, 195
  Central Bank of, 179-80
  cooperative farms in,
  196
  small farmers in, 173-74
Plunkett Foundation for
  Cooperative Studies
  (London), 158
Poland, 206
  cooperative-collective
  farming in, 80-83
  cooperatives in, 196
Production Center Coop-
  eratives (India), 101
Program of Cooperatives
  (of OAS), 199
Puerto Rico, 63, 157, 213

Raiffeisen Association
  (German), 145

Rao, T. S., 129
Reclamation Agricultural
   Cooperative Society, 185
Religions, of developing
   countries, 2, 13
Reserve Bank of India, 99,
   102, 144
Rhodesia, 122
Rural Banks of Mutual
   Credit, 191
Ryukyu Islands, 170,
   178-79

St. Francis University
   (Antigonish, Canada),
   158
Savings, and cooperative
   credit, 86-137
Schiller, Otto, 69
School cooperatives,
   48-51, 201
Self-determination, 7-8
Senegal, 112, 187
Shipe, J. Orrin, 114-15
Sidky, A. R., 141
Siegens, G. St., 35,
   71-72
Sierra Leone, 112, 205
Sociétés de Crédit Mutuel
   (see Sociétés de
   Prévoyance)
Sociétés de Prévoyance
   (Societies of Provident
   Care), 9-12, 111, 120,
   125, 188
Sociétés Mutuelles de
   Production Rurale
   (Mutual Societies of
   Rural Production), 12
Somalia, 6, 129
South America, 59, 63
   (see also individual
   countries)

South Korea, 170, 182,
   194, 195
   constitutional amend-
   ment on cooperatives
   in, 177-78
   cooperative plan of, 173
   savings campaign in, 184
South Vietnam, 146-51,
   170, 177
   Directorate of Coopera-
   tives in, 176
   land resources in, 185-86
   National Agricultural
   Credit Office of, 176
Southeast Asian Seminar
   for Cooperative Insur-
   ance (New Delhi), 136
Special Advisory Committee
   on Cooperatives (of AID),
   27
State Bank of Iran, 143
State Cooperative School
   (Greece), 145
State Reserve Bank of
   India, 99, 102, 144
State socialism, in de-
   veloping countries, 24-25
Suarez, L. A., 157
Subramaniam, C., 195
Sudan, 111-12, 188
Suez Canal, 15
Swedish Cooperative
   Insurance Organization,
   135
Swiss Reinsurance Com-
   pany (Zurich), 135
Syria, 135

Taiwan, 170, 184-85
Tanganyika, 129, 187
   Credit Union League
   of, 193
   (see also Tanzania)

Tanzania (United Republic
   of Tanganyika and
   Zanzibar), 77-79, 190,
   191, 200, 286
Thailand, 74, 128, 135,
   170, 183, 194
   agrarian credit in,
   102, 104-5
   College for Economic
   and Cooperative
   Science, 126
   Cooperative Central
   Bank of, 105
   cooperative efforts,
   and government lead-
   ership in, 25-26
   cooperative legisla-
   tion in, 177
   "group joint liability"
   security in, 181-82
Togo, 11, 120, 187
Trade-union-sponsored
   cooperatives, 198
Trinidad, 127, 128
Troescher, Tassilo, 41
Tunisia, 113, 188
   National Bank of, 187
Tunisian National Agricultural Bank, 190-91
Turkey, 17, 18, 135, 136
   tea exports of, 97

Uganda, 122, 127, 192
   cooperative movements
   in, 124-25
   credit plan in, 192
   rural resistance to
   cooperatives in, 154-55
Unemployment, rural, 46-47
UNESCO (United Nations
   Educational, Scientific
   and Cultural Organiza-
   tion), 142

UNICEF (United Nations
   Children's Emergency
   Fund), 114
Union Cooperative Insurance
   Society (Bombay), 135
United Nations, 160, 194,
   204, 205
United Nations Children's
   Emergency Fund (UNICEF),
   114
United Nations Educational,
   Scientific and Cultural
   Organization (UNESCO),
   142
United Republic of Tan-
   ganyika and Zanzibar
   (see Tanzania)
United States:
   cooperative education
   in, 158
   National Farmers Union,
   30
Upper Volta, 187
Uruguay, 63
Usury, 102-104

Venezuela, 201
Vietnam (see South
   Vietnam)
Vietnam Center, 148
Village Cooperatives, 171
Voorhis, Jerry, 100-101

Waidelich, W., 9, 58, 111,
   145, 151-52
Watkins, W. P., 22-23
West Pakistan, 7
   agricultural coopera-
   tives in, 68-69
   cooperative education
   in, 144, 145

cooperatives in, and
government leadership,
30-31
peasants in, 42
studies of means of
cooperation in, 109-10
(see also Pakistan)
West Pakistan Cooperative
Union, 74
White Highlands (Kenya),
75
WHO (World Health Organi-
zation), 142
Wilbrandt, Hans, 161

Women, rights of, 52
Women's cooperatives,
53-54
Workmen's cooperatives,
46-48, 167
World Bank, 77
World Health Organization
(WHO), 142

Zambia, 190, 191, 200
Zanzibar (see Tanzania)
Zayas-Chardon, Hector, 208

ABOUT THE AUTHOR

Konrad Engelmann has been involved in the international field of cooperative movements for many years. From 1955-63, he served as chief of the foreign relations and related departments of the Central Association of German Rural Cooperatives. Earlier, in Germany, he was a member of the board of executives of the German Central Bank for Cooperatives. In Turkey, from 1936-55, he was an adviser in business management to the Turkish State Enterprises. After he came to the United States in 1946, he worked as the Accounting Director of the National Board of the Young Men's Christian Associations and its affiliations in more than thirty countries.

Mr. Engelmann has traveled widely to Europe, the Near East, and Africa, doing research and work to help the developing countries. He has been at the head of several seminars for cooperators in developing countries and has lectured on cooperatives to various organizations. He is now retired and devotes his time entirely to writing. He contributes regularly to American and German periodicals and has published several books on such topics as credit controls, auditing procedures, and the teaching of business management.